CRIMINOLOGY AND CRIMINAL JUSTICE

Criminal Justice titles available from Butterworth-Heinemann

African American Perspectives on Crime Causation, Criminal Justice Administration, and Crime Prevention
Anne T. Sulton, 0-7506-9813-6

American Jails: Looking to the Future
Kenneth E. Kerle, 0-7506-9846-2

The Art of Investigative Interviewing
Charles L. Yeschke, 0-7506-9808-X

Comparative and International Criminal Justice Systems
Obi N. I. Ebbe, 0-7506-9688-5

Contemporary Criminal Law
David T. Skelton, 0-7506-9811-X

Contemporary Policing: Personnel, Issues, & Trends
M.L. Dantzker, 0-7506-9736-9

Crime & Justice in America: A Human Perspective, Fifth Edition
Territo, Halsted, Bromley, 0-7506-7011-8

Criminal Investigation: Law and Practice
Michael F. Brown, 0-7506-9665-6

Criminal Justice: An Introduction
Philip P. Purpura, 0-7506-9630-3

Criminal Justice Statistics
Lurigio, Dantzker, Seng, Sinacore, 0-7506-9672-9

Criminology and Criminal Justice: Comparing, Contrasting, and Intertwining Disciplines
M.L. Dantzker, 0-7506-9731-8

Death Penalty Cases: Leading U.S. Supreme Court Cases On Capital Punishment
Barry Latzer, 0-7506-9939-6

Introduction to Law Enforcement: An Insider's View
William Doerner, 0-7506-9812-8

The Juvenile Justice System: Law and Process
Mary Clement, 0-7506-9810-1

Practical Applications for Criminal Justice Statistics
Dantzker, Lurigio, Seng, Sinacore, 0-7506-9830-6

CRIMINOLOGY AND CRIMINAL JUSTICE

Comparing, Contrasting, and Intertwining Disciplines

M. L. Dantzker, Ph.D.
Georgia Southern University
Department of Political Science
Justice Studies

Butterworth–Heinemann
Boston   Oxford   Johannesburg   Melbourne   New Delhi   Singapore

141108

Butterworth–Heinemann supports the efforts of American Forests and the Global ReLeaf program in its campaign for the betterment of trees, forests, and our environment.

Library of Congress Cataloging-in-Publication Data
Dantzker, Mark L., 1958–
    Criminology and criminal justice : comparing, contrasting, and
intertwining disciplines / M. L. Dantzker.
        p.   cm.
    Includes bibliographical references and index.
    ISBN 0-7506-9731-8 (pbk.)
    1. Criminology.   2. Criminal justice, Administration of.
I. Title.
HV6030.D36   1998
364—DC21   97-33500
                                                              CIP

British Library Cataloguing-in-Publication Data
A catalogue record for this book is available from the British Library.

The publisher offers special discounts on bulk orders of this book.
For information, please contact:
Manager of Special Sales
Butterworth–Heinemann
225 Wildwood Avenue
Woburn, MA 01801-2041
Tel: 781-904-2500
Fax: 781-904-2620

For information on all Butterworth–Heinemann books available, contact our
World Wide Web home page at: http://www.bh.com

10 9 8 7 6 5 4 3 2 1
Printed in the United States of America

Contents

Preface

Since the 1970s, when criminal justice began to truly emerge as an academic discipline, it has had to compete with criminology and other social science disciplines for respect and students. While the respect has been slow in coming, the students have not. Today there are a number of criminal justice-related programs, including criminology programs, and there are more than 1000 college and university programs catering to over 100,000 students. The popularity of these programs does not appear to be waning. Although criminal justice is growing as a discipline and, if by numbers only, is overshadowing criminology, the presence and purpose of criminology cannot be lost. Therefore, an understanding of both is important.

While the need for both and the distinction between them has not been lost, it has often been limited to discussions among small gatherings at conferences or obscure journal articles. However, as criminal justice education grows, so must criminology because it can be a very important aspect of criminal justice. Furthermore, since both disciplines are important to each other, one might assume that there would be a body of literature that compares and contrasts the two. Yet that does not appear to be the case.

Discussions with colleagues and textbook editors during the 1993 American Society of Criminology's annual conference supported the observation that a book does not exist that examines both criminology and criminal justice from comparative, contrasting, and intertwining perspectives. The overwhelming consensus was that such a book was long overdue. The result of these discussions is this text, *Criminology and Criminal Justice: Comparing, Contrasting, and Intertwining Disciplines.*

This text attempts to fill the void. It describes and discusses criminology and criminal justice as social foci and as academic disciplines. Its comparative and contrasting nature allows readers to gain a better prospective of both ideals as separate entities and also how they are more intertwined than most might recognize or be willing to admit.

Chapter 1, **Foundations,** is the introduction to both ideals as social foci and academic disciplines. It offers an evolutionary view and lays the groundwork for understanding the nature and content. Chapter 2, **Definitions,** offers a variety of definitions for criminology and criminal justice. An extrapolation of the basic elements of each forms the discussion, demonstrating the relationship to both disciplines, to academia, and in practical applications. Chapter 3, **Criminology,** provides an in-depth examination of criminology from a contextual basis using a two-pronged approach. The first is a discussion of the content of criminology as it might be delivered in an introduction to criminal justice course. The second is a fuller discourse of criminology as it might be offered in an introduction to criminology course or within an introduction to criminology textbook. While it discusses the various theories and their general contents, it is not so steeped in theoretical explanation that it represents a full "introduction to criminology" textbook in one chapter. However, it does provide enough information to allow a novice to recognize the breadth of the subject. To balance Chapter 3, **Criminal Justice** is the focus of

Chapter 4. A similar approach is taken, where the content is described as it might be within an introduction to criminal justice course. It provides a broad enough picture of what criminal justice entails, yet is not so detailed as to look like an introduction to criminal justice textbook.

Having established the full foundations of both subjects, the last three chapters are devoted to comparison and application. Chapter 5, **Comparing, Contrasting, and Intertwining,** devotes time to exploring the similarities and differences of criminology and criminal justice as social foci and academic disciplines. Additionally, the discussion looks at how the two can be easily viewed as being more of a singular concept than as two separate concepts. Chapter 6, **Research and Practical Applications,** examines how these two areas can be and are research oriented. Examples of research conducted in both areas are offered. Furthermore, it focuses on the practical applications of criminology to criminal justice and vice versa as well as their combined application to crime-related problems in our communities. Finally, Chapter 7, **The Future,** offers projections for the future of both disciplines as academic and research areas and the importance of their intertwining in both arenas as well as in the practical setting.

Overall, this text suggests that criminology and criminal justice have been, and continue to be, viewed as sharply distinctive entities. Although this is rightly the case, the natural attraction and meshing of the two is emphasized and supported as a future necessity. Ultimately, at the book's conclusion, readers should better understand the similarities and differences of the two as social foci and academic disciplines as well as recognize their singularly distinctive traits.

M. L. Dantzker, Ph.D.

Acknowledgments

Contrary to popular belief, writing a book of any nature is a difficult task and no one should ever have to do it alone. Thankfully, I didn't, and there are people to thank and appreciate. I'll begin with my acquisitions editor, Laurel DeWolf, who for some unknown reason keeps accepting my proposals and forcing me to make good on them. As always, your support was greatly appreciated. I would also like to thank Stephanie Gelman Aronson, Assistant Editor; and Maura Kelly, Production Editor, for their diligence and perseverance in getting this book completed and published; and the reviewers for their insights and astute commentary. Finally, there is my wife, Gail, who, as with all such projects, continues to push, prod, and support. I'm eternally grateful.

Foundations

Crime—whether it is theft, robbery, or murder—has long been a concern of the world's societies. From the earliest recorded histories to today's headlines, crime is an inevitable part of our existence. As such, this has resulted in the scholarly study of related issues that include why people violate the law (or commit crime), the effects of laws, enforcement of the laws, and punishment of those judged to be guilty of violating the law. The study of these and other areas has led to the development of two fields of concentration: criminology and criminal justice.

This chapter addresses the existence and growth of these two dynamic areas of interest. The goal is to establish how both have reached their current status. It will be accomplished through the exploration of the two as social foci and academic disciplines, with a special effort made toward demonstrating how important each is to the other and to society.

ESTABLISHING THE GROUNDWORK

For more than 25 years, universities and colleges have experienced a growth in the number of criminal justice programs. Although an outgrowth of early police-oriented courses developed by Vollmer (Mutchnick, 1989), most criminal justice programs have taken on a character of their own. They have either been practically or academically oriented, or a combination of the two. Furthermore, while criminal justice has grown into its own discipline, a sister discipline, criminology, must be recognized.

Emerging from sociology and older (as an academic discipline) than criminal justice, criminology continues to maintain its existence, but not nearly to the extent of criminal justice. Examination of Anderson Publishing's *Directory of Criminal Justice Programs* finds that the number of criminology programs may not be anywhere close to the number of criminal justice programs.[1] However, criminology as a subject or course has not lost its place in academe or in research. Actually, it may be a very stable component, particularly with respect to the study of criminal justice, which is evidenced in the examination of introduction to criminal justice textbooks. Inevitably, there seems to be at least one section of a chapter, if not several chapters, devoted to the discussion of criminology. Still, it often appears that criminology as an academic discipline has, in some respects, taken a backseat to criminal justice. In particular, criminal justice programs continue to grow, criminal justice research appears more prevalent, publications devoted to criminal justice-related works continue to prosper, and its major organization, the Academy of Criminal Justice Sciences, seems to have surpassed the criminological organization, the American Society of Criminology, in both mem-

---

[1.] An interesting side note is that simply counting programs by their titles may be misleading. In Chapter 5 it is shown how a name may not be a true indicator as to the nature of the program; therefore, the number of criminology programs may be more or even less than the number listed in the directory.

bership and attendance at annual conferences. The apparent rift between the two disciplines is not helped by the long existing, tenuous relationship between those who consider themselves criminologists and those who might best be described as *justicians* (Conrad, 1979; Myren, 1979) or *criminal justice specialists* (Adler, 1995).

Despite the unstable relationship, criminology and criminal justice are intertwining notions, with distinctive differences and comparisons that are "both real and substantive in nature" (Mutchnick, 1989, p. 23). Yet, while this distinction has not been lost on most academics in either field, its exploration does not appear to have gone beyond conference discussions and some obscure journal articles. Still, as criminal justice education grows, so must criminology because it can be a very important aspect of criminal justice, and vice versa. As Pelfrey (1980) states:

> The discipline of criminal justice is viewed by some as being totally separate from the study of criminology. Others view the former as being an integral aspect of the latter. Criminal justice is seen by some as *applied criminology*; for others, it is an area for academic concern on the part of criminologists. Whether the two areas—criminal justice and criminology—are seen as one discipline or two mutually exclusive disciplines, none can rebut the fact that they are closely intertwined. (p. 52)

Since the disciplines are important to each other, one might assume that there would be a body of literature that compares and contrasts the two. Yet that does not appear to be the case. Therefore, it is the goal of this text to provide examination and discussion of criminology and criminal justice as independent, yet codependent, disciplines. To accomplish this, a foundation for each discipline must be set. This will be accomplished through a brief evolutionary discussion of criminology and criminal justice as social foci and as academic disciplines.

EVOLUTIONS

Evolution, according to Funk and Wagnall (1995), is "the act or process of unfolding; development or growth, usually in slow stages and from simpler forms to those [that] are more complex" (p. 441). Criminology and criminal justice have evolved from simple forms to their much more complex forms than one recognizes today. Although the full content of the forms will be discussed in later chapters (3 and 4), before being able to understand that content, we must see where it emerged from. However, be advised that the discussion is limited to the main highlights of evolution because a complete in-depth discussion can and often does require a complete text of its own.[2] Furthermore, this text takes a different approach in that the evolution of criminology and criminal justice are examined as social foci and as academic disciplines. As the older academic discipline, criminology will be explored first.

CRIMINOLOGY—AS A SOCIAL FOCUS

The primary focus of this text is to compare and contrast the disciplines of criminal justice and criminology. To accomplish this task, it requires a brief knowledge of how they became disciplines, which first requires examination of both as social foci.

As previously noted, criminology, as a formal field of study, has existed longer than criminal justice. Pelfrey (1980) advised: "Criminology, as a social focus, emerged with the publication of Cesare Beccaria's *Essay on Crimes and Punishment* in 1764" (p. 1). Beccaria was a utilitarian who believed that a human being was generally a rational being who sought pleasure and tried desperately to avoid pain (Beccaria, 1963). His

---

[2] For example, see Pelfrey (1980), *The Evolution of Criminology* and Johnson and Wolfe (1996), *History of Criminal Justice* (2nd edition). Full citations can be found in the bibliography.

writings were in response to punishment during this time, which was of an extreme nature. It included torture, brandings, mutilation, banishment, and death. Based on his stance and writings, the first recognizable criminological approach to criminal behavior and society's response emerged as what is recognized as the classical school of criminology.

The main claim of the classical school was that crime could be controlled by punishing identified offenders in a way that would make potential offenders fearful of the consequences of committing crime. The main tenets of the classical school were:

1. Social contract—coined by Beccaria as an idea that an individual is bound to society only by his or her own consent and, therefore, society was responsible to him or her
2. Free will—individuals made their own choices to act
3. Seek pleasure and avoid pain
4. Punishment should be used as a deterrent to criminal behavior
5. Identical punishments for identical crimes

Overall, the classical school insisted upon a clear-cut legal definition of the act punishable as criminal and fostering the idea of free will: People commit crimes because of free choice of right or wrong. The classical school of thought would maintain strength and prominence until the 1930s, when it began to decline because of a more treatment-oriented approach fostered by the positive school of criminological thought (additional contributors and aspects of the classical school will be offered in Chapter 3).

Beginning around the late 1800s, a second school of thought would emerge in criminology. Popularly recognized as the positive school of criminology, its humble beginnings are often attributed to an Italian physician, Cesare Lombroso. This school of thought is believed to have emerged "in opposition to the harshness of the classical school, as well as in response to the lack of concern for the causes of criminal behavior" (Pelfrey, 1980, p. 5).

Members of the positive school of thought believed that external forces caused criminal behavior, biological, psychological, and sociological in nature. They rejected the judicial concept of crime recognized by the classical school. Their focus, in search of differences between criminal and noncriminal beings, included the individual instead of the law and a quest for scientific status. That is, why did the behavior occur? A major shift from the classical school was the emphasis on treatment as opposed to punishment. The main tenets of the positive school included:

1. Denial of the free-will concept
2. Multiple causes of criminal behavior
3. Causes are biological and environmental
4. Using scientific methods to look at causes
5. Actions toward the criminal should be to correct the behavior, not punish it

Although three individuals—Cesare Lombroso, Enrico Ferri, and Raffaele Garofalo—are recognized as the impetus behind positivism (often called the "Holy Three of Criminology"), Lombroso is the one who wears the mantle of "Father of Positive Criminology."

Lombroso's ideas arose from his study of cadavers of executed criminals, trying to determine scientifically if there was a positive correlation between physique and crime. It was Lombroso's contention that criminals were physically different from individuals with conventional values and behaviors. Lombroso's theory of criminal behavior included four types of criminals:

1. **Born criminals**—referred to as crimogenic, these individuals had inherited physical problems that led them to commit serious offenses

2. **Atavistic criminals**—these individuals suffered from physical anomalies such as large jaws and canine-type teeth
3. **Insane criminals**—these individuals suffered from various hereditary problems, deafness, venereal diseases, as well as environmental problems such as alcoholism or lack of education
4. **Others**—this group included those who were drawn into crime because of greed or passion or who were only occasionally criminal

Overall, Lombroso's theory was heavily rooted in physical and biological ideology. Despite the large following he had, his theories, along with most of those fostered under the positive school, seem to have very little support or value today primarily because they have not been scientifically proven. (As with the classical school, further discussion of the positive school will be offered in Chapter 3.)

Despite its limited application and lack of scientific support, the positive school remained a mainstay of criminological theory and research into the 1970s because of its psychological and sociological thrusts. However, by the 1970s and continuing today, the classical school has had somewhat of a resurgence. This is because of the disenchantment with the positive school of thought (primarily because of the scientific inability to support its theories), rehabilitation did not seem to work, and the continuing increases in criminal behavior. Notwithstanding its alleged comeback, the classical school of thought does not appear to have done much for criminological theory but has led to additional approaches or schools of thought.

The classical school was concerned with application of law and punishment, and the positive school claimed that biological, psychological and sociological factors affected behavior. By the 1970s, a new response to crime, recognized as the radical school of thought, emerged. The emphasis of this school was that society by itself was the major problem because the powerful in society controlled the nonpowerful. From this school, theories on conflict, Marxism, group, and social reality would develop and continue to receive attention. Most recently, a contemporary school of thought is developing that includes focusing on specific group impact, such as female criminality. (Again, Chapter 3 explores these last two schools of thought in greater detail.)

In short, criminology as a social focus has existed in some form or fashion for more than 200 years. Yet, despite its longevity as a social focus, its existence as an academic discipline is much shorter.

CRIMINOLOGY—AS AN ACADEMIC DISCIPLINE

As a social focus, it has been noted that criminology has existed for about 200 years. Its existence as an academic discipline is nowhere near as old.

Unlike its sister discipline, criminal justice, the actual emergence of criminology as its own discipline is much more difficult to pinpoint. For many years, criminology had been a subdiscipline of sociology (and in some cases, still is!). The majority of criminologists were sociologists who studied crime and its societal relationships. A review of the literature finds that criminology began to build its road to separatism from sociology in the 1950s. Identified as a catalyst for this drive and "a major landmark in criminology" (Pelfrey, 1980, p. 13) was C. Ray Jeffery's *The Structure of American Criminological Thinking* (1956), where Jeffery conducted a critical analysis of criminology. Despite the significance of this work, the truer emergence of criminology appears to have begun in the late 1960s as sociology and other social sciences were undergoing criticisms and change. (Note: This was about the time that "radical" criminology began emerging as a field of study.)

It is observed that about this time, criminology (and criminologists) was offered a challenge to become progressive and mature into its own science (Reasons, 1974). With sociology facing its own identity crisis, it was only natural that criminology would begin to pull away and become its own discipline. To date, criminology is still struggling to maintain its individuality. Nevertheless, it continues to face challenges from waning sociology departments needing an infusion that criminology and its majors can bring and by criminal justice programs that are continuing to flourish because of its links to employment in the criminal justice system. Regardless of its stance as a discipline, it remains an important aspect of the study of crime and criminal behavior and thus links to criminal justice. In essence, we can view criminology as the scientific study of criminal behavior as it pertains to criminal justice, the social focus.

CRIMINAL JUSTICE—AS A SOCIAL FOCUS

While criminology may be older with respect to academic nature and application, it is easily arguable that criminal justice as a social focus is much older. Unlike criminology's social focus as a theoretical approach to addressing and understanding crime, criminal behavior, law, and punishment, criminal justice's social focus is really a historic examination of the applied aspect of law and punishment. Ultimately, criminal justice as a social focus deals with the creation, application, and enforcement of criminal laws to maintain social order.

Despite knowing that the term *history* often turns many students off because of their perceptions that "history is boring," a brief historical accounting of the growth of criminal justice is important toward understanding it as an academic discipline. Besides, as Johnson and Wolfe (1996) suggest:

1. History makes available a sound perspective concerning the nature of human growth and development.
2. Historical knowledge brings with it some assurance against "reinventing the wheel."
3. History demands critical analysis and careful thought from its students (p. 2).

To truly understand criminal justice as a discipline, knowing its history as a social focus is a necessity.

History of Criminal Justice

The history of criminal justice dates from ancient times with biblical Israel, the Greeks, and Romans (Johnson & Wolfe, 1996). This is where the foundations for criminal justice are first laid, with all three cultures offering the establishment of strict laws and swift, harsh punishment. However, for this text, the evolution we are most interested in does not truly begin until the colonization of America.

Beginning with colonization, criminal justice in America has seen many changes, transitioning from harsh and swift punishment to provisions of strong constitutional rights, rehabilitation, and more appropriately applied punishments. This transition includes the development of modern policing, more acceptable jails and prisons, separation of juveniles from adults, more lenient sentencing and punishments, and enforcement of constitutional guarantees. The evolution of these aspects and their representative institutions has led to the recognition of the system of criminal justice. Yet seldom can the system itself be understood without closer examination of its three main components: police, courts, and corrections. The following is a brief overview of each component's evolution.

Police

As the most recognizable and observable component in the criminal justice system (CJS), policing has experienced a myriad of changes. Nowhere is this more evident than in the review of police evolution from a role perspective. To demonstrate the transition, the police role timeline continuum, which is divided into six overlapping divisions, is employed (Dantzker, 1995).

Starting with colonial America (1700s–1820s), policing was primarily the role of reactive crime fighters. The basic institutions were the sheriff, the constable, and the watch, which were the result of English heritage. The two main traits were limited authority and local control. Selection criteria and training were practically nonexistent. All comers volunteered or served at the whim of the political leadership. Malfeasance and corruption were highly recognizable elements.

Moving into the preindustrial era (1820s–1850s), the first movement toward modernization of policing was witnessed. Although the role was still predominantly one of reactive crime fighter, thanks to the creation of the London Metropolitan Police Department, American cities now had a model to use for implementing "real" police departments. Boston, New York, and Philadelphia were among the first cities to create full-fledged police agencies. Crime prevention and preventive patrol would be the key characteristics of these new police agencies.

The 1850s to 1920s, labeled as industrial America, is best described as the infancy of policing, whose role was still crime fighter but now with a proactive description. The Industrial Revolution and World War I were two major factors leading to a need to stabilize the police role.

> In general, the reception to police development was good. However, this period produced an extremely politically active climate in this country, particularly for policing. Every major aspect of policing—personnel standards, recruitment, policy priorities, and corruption—was tremendously influenced by politics. In some cases this is still true today, particularly in the area of personnel. (Dantzker, 1995, p. 12)

Despite the need for a more stable police role, efforts to achieve this were plagued by irresponsibility, public disrespect, a lack of professionalism, and, most specifically, corruption. Needless to say, this was not a simple period for police development and was, in fact, the impetus for major changes.

In terms of modernization, the 1920s–1960s provided the most activity. Technological developments and implementation into policing—such as the automobile, telephone, and radio—helped the proactive crime fighter become mobile. Yet this was not enough to stimulate true change from the corrupt, ill-trained police. This transition can be attributed to other sources, such as the Wickersham Commission (the first national effort to study criminal justice and policing), efforts of individuals like August Vollmer and O. W. Wilson, who fervently pushed for better training and education among police recruits, and the Federal Bureau of Investigation's professional development under J. Edgar Hoover. Due to the various influences the "role of a well-trained, educated crime fighter was becoming recognizable" (Dantzker, 1995, p. 15).

By the 1960s the social changes that had been taking place in this country would come to the forefront and would be the beginning of "Crisis America" (1960s–1980s). Civil unrest due to the striving for civil rights and protest against the Vietnam War, several landmark U.S. Supreme Court decisions, recommendations from another national commission (President's Commission on Law Enforcement and the Administration of Justice) and the resulting federal legislation creating the Law Enforcement Assistance Administration, and the changes in youth's approach to society (sex, the drug and music revolutions) would cause the police role to take a new turn, from crime fighting to being more order-maintenance and social-service oriented. This timeframe would see millions of dollars injected into police education, training, and research in an effort to improve how the police dealt with the public and society's needs.

> Policing made it through the 1960s and 1970s with a relatively new and more stable idea of its role. During the remainder of the 1970s, policing saw the growth of police unionism, higher educational requirements, and affirmative action in hiring. It also saw a transition in the police role. Crime fighting was often no longer the primary activity simply because society required more from its police than being crime fighters. The growing need for the police to be social service and order maintenance oriented was imperative to society and the police role. (Dantzker, 1995, p. 17)

By the 1980s, the police role had become more apparent and fixed with technology—again, helping job tasks get accomplished. However, it helped shape the current role of policing as a multifaceted social servant whose role is viewed as being "everything to everyone."

Today the police are often looked to for aid or assistance for any problem that arises where it is not obvious as to who else one should call. A negative result is that police have not been able to attend to crime problems nearly as much as society seems to want them to. Furthermore, despite improvements in selection and training, the police still face serious questions about their activities and responses to certain situations, such as use of excessive force, domestic violence, or violating constitutional rights. Obviously, the evolution continues.

Courts

Unlike policing, the evolution of the courts was more consistent and stable. Like policing, the earliest roots are found in ancient civilizations, and America's start is distinctively English rooted. As Holten and Lamar (1991) noted,

> By the time colonization of North America became a primary goal of British policy, the legal and court system of the mother country was firmly established. It therefore provided the foundation for the American system, if only because it was the only system with which most colonists were familiar. (p. 46)

Starting with the courts in colonial America, it's been said:

> [The] courts in colonial America had varied and nebulous beginnings. They came into being in an assortment of ways, including specific authorization by the king in royal charters, acts of governors exercising royal prerogative, and legislation by colonial assemblies. The English government permitted a range of experiments, insisting only that colonial law not controvert English law. (Holten & Lamar, 1991, pp. 46–47)

By the time the Declaration of Independence took effect, the royal courts had been replaced with courts authorized by acts of assemblies. While the new courts varied by state on how they were created (by constitution or from old charters) and the term length for judges and who appointed them, "all the states generally preserved the old organizational principles. Thus there were courts of general trial jurisdiction with civil, criminal, and chancery functions" (Holten & Lamar, 1991, p. 49). The Declaration of Independence and U.S. Constitution gave rise to the federal courts, which had been nonexistent.

Article III of the U.S. Constitution says, "The judicial power of the United States, shall be vested in one supreme court, and in such inferior courts as the congress may from time to time ordain and establish." This allowed the first Congress to pass the Judiciary Act of 1789, "which fleshed out the first true national court system. It provided for circuit and thirteen district courts" (Holten & Lamar, 1991, p. 51). The circuit courts of appeal were created in 1891, and by 1911 the circuit and district trial courts were combined into the three-tier system we recognize today, which consists of 12 circuit and 94 district courts.

Corrections

As regards corrections, the interest is primarily with jails and prisons. With the exception of the growth in numbers of facilities, their designs, and issues associated with housing large numbers of individuals, there has been relatively little change since the late 1700s. The most noticeable change has been in how we punish individuals, evolving from corporal punishment to what is considered more humane, incarceration. However, capital punishment has remained in use despite changes in what it can be used for and how it can be used. The other obvious change has been in the philosophy applied to corrections (which is explored in greater depth in Chapter 4).

Other evolutions affecting the system have dealt with juveniles and other methods of punishment. For juveniles, early history indicates that they were treated the same as adults and often housed with them in correctional facilities. However, by the mid-1800s the approach toward juveniles became more of social concern and well-being than of punishment. The Illinois Juvenile Court Act of 1899 became the model for juvenile statutes throughout the nation, helping to lead to a separate system of justice for juveniles. With the exception of court cases allowing for the application of constitutional rights to juveniles, this portion has remained consistent for the past 90 years.

Parole and probation began in 1822 and 1841, respectively, as means of dealing with convicted persons. Other than the increasing numbers of individuals serving both, there has been little change in these concepts.

Overall, it is clear that the three main components of the CJS have witnessed changes. These changes, occurring at different times, have continued to cause the CJS to be in a constant state of flux. Furthermore, it should be evident that criminal justice as a social focus may be identified as a system but really rests upon the actions of the three main components: police, courts, and corrections. Thus, understanding criminal justice relies upon one's understanding of the CJS's components and their evolutions. Therefore, how this system operates has long become the focus of criminal justice as a discipline.

CRIMINAL JUSTICE— AS AN ACADEMIC DISCIPLINE

As an academic discipline, criminal justice may best be viewed as the study of the creation, application, and enforcement of criminal laws to maintain social order by the primary institutions and agencies working under the guise of police, courts, and corrections. Yet where did this begin? John P. Conrad (1979) noted, "Few watersheds in the history of any discipline can be so precisely dated as the transformation of criminal justice studies under the powerful influence of the Law Enforcement Assistance Administration" (p. 7).

Criminal justice as an academic discipline first began in the early 1900s as police-science courses (but with a strong training approach) offered by August Vollmer at the University of California at Berkeley (Mutchnick, 1989; Pelfrey, 1980). This was followed by a police training program at the University of Chicago in 1929 and similar programs at other institutions. A steady growth of police-related programs continued until the 1960s. The first established program using the term *criminal justice* in its title was in 1966 with the establishment of the SUNYA (State University of New York–Albany) School of Criminal Justice.

> In 1963 Governor Nelson Rockefeller decided to meet the demand for an academic program organized around the issues of crime and its control. In 1966 a cadre of scholars gathered in Albany to create the concepts of the school, under the direction of the first dean, Richard Myren. (SUNY website—Criminal Justice [http://www.suny.edu], 1997, p. 2)

This school's development was a few years before legislation, based on recommendations from the President's Commission on Law Enforcement and the Administration of Justice, that would create the impetus for growth of criminal justice education. This growth of criminal justice as an academic discipline resulted from the creation of the Law Enforcement Assistance Administration (1969), which provided funding to colleges and universities offering criminal justice programs. By 1978 there were more than 1000 programs proffering criminal justice education.

Today, there are approximately 1300 universities and colleges offering a rubric of criminal justice-related programs (for example, criminal justice, criminology, justice studies, administration of justice, law enforcement, et cetera). Yet even with the large number of programs, criminal justice has had a difficult time gaining status as a true academic discipline. This is unlike criminology, whose close ties to sociology allow for its acceptance as an academic discipline. However, criminal justice has earned the right to recognition as a distinct discipline. As Frank Cullen, criminal justice professor and past president of the Academy of Criminal Justice Sciences, has noted (1995), criminal justice has all the hallmarks of an academic discipline:

1. Distinct departments or programs, whose curricula are instructed fully by criminal justice faculty
2. Ph.D. programs dedicated to the creation of criminal justice knowledge and to the scholarly training of researchers, most of whom will assume academic positions
3. Numerous scholarly journals dedicated exclusively to the publication and the transmission of criminal justice knowledge
4. Separate professional organizations dedicated to the dissemination of criminal justice knowledge through scholarship and education
5. A rapidly expanding knowledge base, which increasingly is produced by scholars trained by or working in departments of criminal justice
6. A large student population who define themselves as "criminal justice majors"
7. Faculty whose academic identity is criminal justice (p. 3)

Still, despite the above identified hallmarks, criminal justice continues to struggle to achieve full acceptance by its social science counterparts as well as academic administrators. Nevertheless, it has become an extremely popular field of study for students, particularly those interested in pursuing employment in the criminal justice system. Of course, this may be one of the problems in the lack of acceptance of criminal justice as a true academic discipline.

Unlike most other social sciences, including its sister, criminology, criminal justice has a dual role: as a social science field of study and as semipreparation for employment in the criminal justice field. Because its focus of study is the same system in which students can gain employment, it lends to its popularity as an academic major. The downside is that students, practitioners, and academicians all believe that by completing a degree program in criminal justice, the student is being trained for a specific job in criminal justice. This is a fallacy that has been difficult to eliminate.

During the earlier days of criminal justice as police science or law enforcement, the emphasis was on training or educating by police practitioners who told "war stories." It was quite common for students in these programs to take courses on self-defense, report writing, first aid, patrol techniques, and so on that were geared toward preparing the student for entry into law enforcement.

While the focus of many criminal justice programs has gone away from the applied approach toward a more theoretical approach, the subject matter by itself is inundated with an applied nature. Thus, it has been very difficult for criminal justice to be accepted as a true academic discipline. However, it should become quite clear by book's end that while the evolution continues, criminal justice is a strong, viable discipline whose existence is necessary and vital to criminology—and vice versa.

CONCLUSION

Criminology and criminal justice are divergent yet similar ideas that exist as social foci and academic disciplines. As a social focus, criminology relates to criminal behavior and treatment, a concern that has existed for over 200 years. On the other hand, criminal justice deals with the structure and application of those entities that must deal with the criminal behavior. Its very nature has been documented to be literally thousands of years in the making. Yet despite the difference in ages of existence, criminology and criminal justice as social foci revolve around the same core: crime.

As an academic discipline, criminology is theoretically based as an outgrowth of sociology and is still trying to fully establish itself as a solid and separate discipline. Criminal justice has evolved from more applied programs of police science or law enforcement and is half the age of criminology, yet it appears to have become a much more popular academic discipline, at least among college students interested in employment in the CJS.

In either case, both are necessary parts of society and academe. Furthermore, there is an apparent intertwining relationship, and it is necessary to provide a venue where comparison, contrast, intertwinement, and application can be examined.

FOR THE CRITICAL THINKER

1. Differentiate criminology as a social focus from that of an academic discipline. How different are they?
2. From an evolutionary perspective, which deserves more attention, criminology or criminal justice? Where should greater focus be placed today? Why?
3. If one scrutinizes both criminology and criminal justice as social foci, it is relatively clear how closely linked they are. Describe that link. Explain why it has not received more attention than what has been noted.
4. Apparently, criminal justice is an important social focus and academic area in our society. Discuss why it is that we try to separate them. Should a social focus become a field of study? Why?
5. What might be a better way to describe the evolution of criminology and criminal justice other than as social foci or academic disciplines? How important is the ability to describe the evolutions in any manner?

2

Definitions

In the previous chapter, an introduction was made to two concepts: criminology and criminal justice. To study and understand any concept, it always helps to have a definition from which to begin. For criminology and criminal justice, finding a definition to begin with is very simple; agreeing about which one is not. A plethora of definitions can be found for both concepts. It seems as if every criminology and criminal justice textbook written offers a definition. Occasionally, a definition of each can be found in the same text.

The reason for this phenomenon might best be addressed through the words of J. P. Conrad (1979) who stated that "Many writers have striven for a version they could call their own—precise, including only the necessary and sufficient elements, and excluding everything extraneous" (p. 9). I will be among those writers who will offer his own definitions for both criminology and criminal justice. However, the intent is not to suggest that these definitions are better, rather that they might best summarize the key components extrapolated from many previously

existing definitions. Therefore, this chapter provides several definitions for both subjects. It will extrapolate the basic elements
into generic, global definitions. Finally, it will explore the relativity to each other, academia, research, and practical applications.

CRIMINOLOGY

As previously noted, every criminology text and most criminal
justice texts offer a definition of criminology. The use of the following examples helps to extrapolate terms and create the working definition for this text. It begins with what has been described
as a definition that "opens the most famous criminological text
and serves to mark off the territory" (Conrad, 1979, p. 9).

> Criminology is the body of knowledge regarding crime as a
> social phenomenon. It includes within its scope the pro-
> cesses of making laws, of breaking laws, and of reacting
> toward the breaking of laws. These processes are three
> aspects of a somewhat unified sequence of interactions. Cer-
> tain acts [that] are regarded as undesirable are defined by
> the political society as crimes. In spite of this definition,
> some people persist in the behavior and thus commit
> crimes; the political society reacts by punishment, treat-
> ment, or prevention. This sequence of interactions is the
> object-matter of criminology. (Sutherland & Cressey, 1960,
> p. 3)

While the remaining definitions could all be considered
outgrowths of Sutherland and Cressey's definition, one should
note a major aspect in the other definitions, and missing from
Sutherland and Cressey's is the addition of "scientific study or
approach." Therefore, criminology has also been defined as:

> The study of the causes of crime and criminal motivation. It
> combines the academic disciplines of sociology and psy-
> chology in an effort to explore the mind of the offender; the
> scientific study of crime causation, prevention, and the

rehabilitation and punishment of offenders (Schmalleger, 1996, p. 13; 1997, p. 28);

The scientific approach to the study of the nature, extent, cause, and control of criminal behavior (Senna and Siegel, 1996, p. 4);

A discipline that scientifically examines crime and criminal behavior, including forms of criminal behavior, the causes of crime, and the societal reaction to crime (Champion, 1990, p. 4);

The study of . . . the phenomenon . . . and of the factors or circumstances—individual or environmental—[that] may have an influence on, or be associated with, criminal behavior and the state of crime in general (Waldron, 1989, p. 4);

The scientific study of crime and criminal behavior; the body of knowledge regarding crime as a social phenomenon, largely concerned with finding "causes" of criminal behavior and measuring the extent of crime (Newman and Anderson, 1989, p. 674);

Modern criminology is the academic field of study that uses naturalistic reasoning to investigate the following issues: How are definitions of criminal and delinquent behavior derived? What are the causes of criminal and delinquent behavior? and How should society respond to criminal and delinquent behavior (Levine, Musheno, and Palumbo, 1986, p. 126); and,

As a discipline is concerned with the development of a body of knowledge regarding the making of laws, the breaking of laws, and society's reaction to the breaking of laws (Pelfrey, 1980, p. 51).

In considering the content of the definitions given, a simplistic yet straightforward defining of criminology is achievable. However, before establishing or accepting a new working definition, an exploration of the elements of the other definitions is appropriate.

Definitional Elements

Through the analysis of the various definitions cited, four common elements are observed

- Crime as a social phenomenon
- Scientific study or approach
- Criminal behavior
- Causes of or influences on criminal behavior

Crime as a Social Phenomenon

With respect to crime as a social phenomenon, Sutherland noted that criminology "is the body of knowledge" that relates to crime in this capacity. As a phenomenon, it is "something visible or directly observable, as an appearance, action, change, or occurrence of any kind, as distinguished from the force by which, or the law in accordance with which it may be produced" (Funk & Wagnall, 1995, p. 947). Crime is that which legislative bodies define as activities or failures to act (omission) that are unlawful. By participating in such an activity or failure to act (omission), an individual has committed a crime. The first element of the definition of criminology advises that it offers information about why crime exists, particularly the extent to which it occurs. Nevertheless, there is no consensus whether the information is absolute, thus leading to the theoretical basis of this knowledge—in other words, the provision of theories.

The root of this first element is made up by the theoretical foundations or theories that compose the body of knowledge. As such, what, then, is a theory? Very plainly, a theory is a part of an explanation—which leads to the question, What is an explanation? An explanation is a sensible relating of some particular phenomenon to the whole field of knowledge. Therefore, one could say that a usable element for defining criminology is the offering of theories or explanations about why crime occurs, why it is the social phenomenon that it is.

Scientific Study or Approach

Probably the most difficult or controversial element in these definitions is the use of scientific study or approach. In the context of social sciences, where criminology finds itself, the concept of scientific study is often difficult for many social scientists to accept. For centuries, scientific study has been associated with the natural sciences or medicine in that it has often applied to the ability to test or experiment. Within the social sciences, testing or experimentation is often extremely difficult because what one often tests is a hypothesis, an educated guess about why something is the way it is or does what it does. It has been pointed out that much has been written about the scientific approach (Conrad, 1979). As a result, Conrad's simple but competent definition was chosen to explain this method: "The scientific method consists of the generation of hypotheses for the explanation of perceived phenomenon and the search for the most reliable evidence to confirm or falsify these hypotheses" (1979, p. 9). Applying this to the definition of criminology extends the idea that criminology uses this approach to try to understand crime, which is that it offers hypotheses, usually in the guise of theories, to explain this social phenomenon.

If one accepts that criminology is a scientific study of crime, then we must accept that there are scientific theories. A scientific theory is best viewed as a one-of-a-kind explanation that generally makes a statement, which one may dispute, about the relationship between two types of phenomena. The outcome is to provide a theory that truly can explain the phenomenon in question. However, it has been advised that there are only two types of theories: spiritual and natural.

The followers of the notion of spiritual theories have a general view of life in which occurrences and events are believed to be influenced by otherworldly powers. This notion is rooted in early beliefs of satanic possession and witchcraft, which led to sacrifices or trials by battle or ordeal. Although these theories may have offered consolation to some individuals, because they cannot be disproved, they cannot be given any plausibility.

On the other hand, natural theorists tend to explain what happens through the use of objects and events. For example, Hippocrates used physiological causes, while Socrates, Plato, and Aristotle argued the influence of the physical and material to explain criminal behavior. Obviously there is no consensus among natural theorists, except that spiritual theories are nonsense. The result is three ways of viewing crime from a natural perspective:

1. Criminal behavior is freely chosen; that is, individuals choose to commit criminal behavior, supporting the classical school's idea of free will.
2. Criminal behavior is caused; that is, it can be determined by factors that are beyond an individual's controls such as biological, psychological, or sociological cause (mainstays of the positive school of thought).
3. Behavior of criminal law, which concentrates on why laws are defined as such and their effects (a component of the radical school of thought).

No matter what theory is followed, the ability to examine it through scientific methodology is the key. To accomplish this, there must be a consensus about how to examine it and why. The "how" will be examined later in the chapter. The "why" is criminal behavior.

Criminal Behavior

A consistent element among the definitions is criminal behavior. Basically, this is a blanket description for those activities or omissions associated with a given crime. Criminology is interested in understanding why individuals will risk being caught committing these activities or omissions and being labeled criminal. Additionally, it attempts to explain why people may commit this behavior. In retrospect, this element is easily a subelement of crime as a social phenomenon. Then again, so is the last element.

Causes or Influences

The heart of the definitions of criminology tends to involve the ability to explain what causes or influences individuals to partake in criminal behavior. It is this last element that has become one of the main thrusts of criminology. A number of hypotheses have been offered as to why individuals commit crime, the majority of which stem from within the three schools of thought introduced in the first chapter and to be more fully explored in the following chapter.

Clearly, the examination of various definitions provides us with at least four common elements that create the foundations for defining criminology. Yet two of those elements, criminal behavior and causes or influences, could easily be considered subcategories to crime as a social phenomenon. Therefore, the following simple yet straightforward defining of criminology is presented:

> Criminology is the scientific approach to the study of crime as a social phenomenon; that is, it is the *theoretical* application involving the study of the nature and extent of *criminal behavior*.

It is from this perspective that other aspects of this text will be related. Furthermore, it coincides and reflects well upon the definition proposed in the previous chapter. Having established a working definition, we can now take the exploration of criminology, still from a definitional perspective, one step further.

Working from the newest definition, it can be said that a major objective of criminology is developing general and testable principles. These principles are intended to be used as building blocks for the body of knowledge relating to the process of law, crime, punishment, and treatment. To accomplish this, criminology must call upon other social sciences such as anthropology, biology, economics, history, sociology, psychology, and political science, which tends to give criminology a multidisciplinary persona. To meet the objective, several issues may be studied. They include:

1. The creation and use of laws in society—Why do we create certain laws? Who are they created for or against? Are they applied fair and equitably? These are just a few of the concerns associated with this issue.
2. Examination of the patterns of crime—Interests include who commits crime (age, gender, race), where and when crimes are committed, what trends can be identified whether by crime type, geography, economics, and so on.
3. Causation of crime and criminality—What influences this behavior (environment, genetics, social development, and the like)?
4. Societal response and reaction to criminality—Revenge, vigilantism, purchasing protective devices or services are examples of how society responds and reacts to crime that criminology is interested in understanding.
5. The administration of justice—How fair and equitable the police, courts, and corrections are is an important aspect to the concerns associated with this issue to criminology.
6. Custody and punishment of those accused and convicted of criminality—How do we treat those who end up in jails and prisons, those who must partake in community service, or any of the other means used to deal with the accused and convicted?
7. Treatment or rehabilitation of those labeled criminal— Are we successful? Why do we fail? Can it be accomplished? These are just a few questions for which answers are sought.

141108

In this regard, criminology has come a long way toward building a general body of knowledge that focuses on social norms (rules, law), deviance (norm violations), and social control. Yet despite the efforts of the discipline as a whole, individuals who study criminology—generally called criminologists—cannot reach an agreement as to (a) what should be studied, (b) who can apply the knowledge gathered, and (c) what ultimately should be achieved by the knowledge attained. The result of this disagreement has led to three speciality areas of criminological study:

1. **Sociology of law,** which is the understanding of how laws are created and enacted, modified, and applied
2. **Criminological theory,** which focuses on those who violate the law and why
3. **Penology,** which is the study of punishment

Ultimately, despite the simplistic attempt to define criminology as a discipline, it is much more complex than indicated. This complexity will become clearer in Chapter 3. Still, if we accept criminology as the theoretical approach, what is criminal justice?

CRIMINAL JUSTICE

Considering the plethora of definitions found for criminology, it is conceivable that the same can be true for criminal justice. Yet possibly because it is so much newer than criminology as a bonafide field of study, we still have not completely decided what criminal justice is, and thus definitions are still relatively limited. Still, there are enough attempts to define criminal justice that we find ourselves in a somewhat similar predicament as with criminology. For criminal justice, here are examples of these definitions:

> Criminal justice focuses on the criminal law, the law of criminal procedure, and the enforcement of these laws, in

an effort to treat fairly all persons accused of a crime (Purpura, 1997, p. 3).

Criminal justice, in its broadest sense, refers to those aspects
of social justice [that]concern violations of the criminal law
(Schmalleger, 1997, p. 14).

A scientific approach to understanding the primary functions of the criminal justice system; its influence on human
behavior and how it is influenced by society.[1]

An interdisciplinary field that studies the nature and operations of organizations providing justice services to society
(Champion, 1990, p. 4).

Mostly concerned with the decision process in the crime
control agencies of police, prosecutors' offices, trial courts,
and correctional facilities, and in programs like probation
and parole (Pelfrey, 1980, p. 51).

The exploration of these definitions apparently does not
offer as easy a task of identifying common elements. Yet one common trait is apparent: Criminal justice is a process for dealing
with the law. Still, it seems that there is more to criminal justice.
The definitional result favors a general, summarized "working"
definition of criminal justice that has been previously used in an
introductory criminal justice course and is employed for the duration of this text:

Criminal justice is the applied and scientific study of the
practical applications of criminal behavior; that is, the
actions, policies, or functions of the *agencies* within the criminal justice system charged with addressing this behavior.

---

[1] Since I have used this definition for many years, during which time I have redone my
notes several times, I have forgotten its source. However, I do not claim it as my own.

Using this definition, a more in-depth definitional discussion of criminal justice can be offered.

From a Definitional Perspective

One of the most interesting aspects of criminal justice from a definitional perspective centers around the debate about whether criminal justice is an applied or a social science. Because many who study and contribute to criminal justice are practitioners, and earlier programs were more training oriented, there has long been a shadow over criminal justice. This shadow has carried the description of "applied." This means that what individuals teach or study in criminal justice is something that can be put into practice or utilized in a way that something abstract or pure could not, such as a theory derived within a social-science setting like that found in criminology.

For many years, criminal justice programs have tried to cast aside the shadow of being an applied science by eliminating the "practical or applied" courses, such as report writing, traffic law, even criminal investigations, and by increasing the theoretical approach to the study of the practical side of criminal justice. This has meant taking a stronger methodological approach to understanding and teaching about the center of criminal justice—the criminal justice system.

The criminal justice system consists of the practical components—police, courts, and corrections—that are charged with responding to those accused of committing criminal behavior. Analyzing, studying, and observing how these components carry out their tasks is the mainstay of criminal justice as a discipline. Since these components are very much the practical side of criminal justice, antagonists argue that this makes criminal justice an applied science, especially when one factors in that many students who major in criminal justice do so because of their desire to become employed in the criminal justice system (CJS).

Advocates, however, argue that employment is simply one positive quirk of the discipline and claim that criminal justice is a social science that focuses on the CJS components and their behavior in an attempt to explain how and why they function as they do, just as criminology attempts to explain why criminal behavior exists. Like criminologists, justicians often use scientific methods to discover answers. The fact that criminal justice, by nature, has both an applied and a social-science slant should cause one to conclude that criminal justice is an applied social science, thus the cause for the working definition previously offered. Unfortunately, this conclusion will not eliminate the debate as to whether criminal justice is an applied or social science, but it does allow for what is believed to be a more rational approach to defining it.

Obviously, defining criminal justice is not as clear-cut as defining criminology. Still, the working definitions brought forth are definitive enough to allow for further exploration and understanding of the two topics, which can include comparing and contrasting from the academic, research, and practical perspectives (Chapters 5 and 6).

CONCLUSION

To begin to understand any concept, it helps to be able to define it. Criminal justice and criminology are no exception. A number of acceptable definitions exist for both, leading to a need for a simple yet straightforward definitional compromise. Therefore, this text offers that *criminology is the scientific approach to the study of crime as a social phenomenon; that is, the theoretical application involving the study of the nature and extent of criminal behavior* and *criminal justice is the applied and scientific study of the practical applications of criminal behavior; that is, the actions, policies, or functions of the agencies within the criminal justice system charged with addressing this behavior.*

From these definitions we discover that both purport to use a scientific method of study. Their primary emphasis is the study of criminal behavior. Where they differ is that criminological study is primarily theory oriented in that it looks for the whys and wherefores of criminal behavior. In contrast, criminal justice is interested in the system and its components' responses to the criminal behavior. Still, the fact remains that both center on crime and criminal behavior, which provides the first true link between the two disciplines.

Additionally, while the working definitions attempt to distinctively separate each discipline, there are underlying crosscurrents. For example, criminology can offer practical application to the study of crime and behavior (say, following gang activities in an effort to document members' behaviors and patterns of behavior). Similarly, criminal justice can attempt to theorize why certain aspects of the system do not function well or do not address criminal behavior in a manner expected (say, a study of correctional officers' interactions with inmates).

In either case, both try to explain and deal with criminal behavior. In so doing, perhaps the linkage is stronger than some might wish to recognize, even from a definitional perspective. Later discussions will champion this thought and provide further support that there are stronger links between the two than what is readily observable.

FOR THE CRITICAL THINKER

1. In examining the definitions provided, how would you define criminology? Criminal justice?
2. It is clear that definitions of criminology share some common traits. Among definitions for criminal justice, the identification of similar traits is not as easy. You have been mandated to identify three common characteristics or traits of criminal justice definitions. What are they?
3. Simply based on the definitions offered, could one definition be formed that describes both criminal justice and criminology? Why? Try to create a singular definition for criminology and criminal justice.

4. Assume that criminology and criminal justice have been merged into one concept. Define it.
5. It was argued that the newness of criminal justice as an academic field precludes a standardized definition. Is it the time of existence or simply the "nature of the beast" that influences the definitional quandary? How?

Criminology

3

Having set the foundation and defined the concept, we can now explore the content of criminology. Since criminology is more readily recognized as an academic discipline, to better understand it, we will examine its content as it might exist within the confines of the classroom or within an introductory criminology textbook. Therefore, the perspective or approach taken in this chapter is one that is believed to better facilitate the introduction of the content of criminology, regardless of the arena or venue it is offered in. However, since teaching is the mainstay, this perspective must be addressed.

FROM A TEACHING PERSPECTIVE

It has been stated, "Criminology is one of the most frequently taught courses in the standard undergraduate sociology curriculum" (Rogers, 1986, p. 275). Introduction to Criminology is also the first course that students seeking to major in criminology must take. Furthermore, most criminal justice academicians would probably agree that Introduction to Criminology is among the more frequently taught subjects in a criminal justice curriculum, too.

As an important course, with respect to the disciplines mentioned, there are a number of textbooks available that pertain specifically to criminology from an introductory perspective. Despite the number of texts, there is very little difference as to the content; only the presentation may differ. As a result, while teaching styles also differ, the teaching of criminology has been cited as "among the most challenging to teach" (Rogers, 1986, p. 257). This is particularly true for those instructors who might not have a strong criminological background. This chapter offers two contextual approaches for understanding criminology from a teaching perspective. The first responds to teaching criminology within the confines of an introductory criminal justice course,[1] and the second is suggested content for an introduction to criminology course.

CRIMINOLOGY WITHIN CRIMINAL JUSTICE

Instructors with a strong criminological background may have little to no problem teaching a complete introductory criminology course. However, some instructors may find that teaching criminology within the confines of an introductory criminal justice course is not easy, especially when one wants students to get a good feel for the subject—at least enough to "whet their appetites" and perhaps create a desire for further knowledge in this area. Therefore, to satisfy all those concerned the following approach to teaching criminology in a criminal justice course is suggested.

[1.] At this juncture I'd like to point out that this is an interesting dilemma. While criminology is taught (albeit in a limited way) within a criminal justice course, seldom, if ever, is criminal justice taught within the confines of a criminology course.

The course can begin by advising students that criminology offers theories, concepts, and explanations about criminal behavior, emphasizing the theory aspect. While these theories could conceivably influence actions in the criminal justice system, such as a judge's sentence or a jury's verdict, it could be contended that they ultimately have little influence on the behavior of actors in the criminal justice system. One reason for this approach is that criminology offers a plethora of untested, unproven, possible explanations for criminal behaviors that are extremely difficult to apply in a practical manner. However, a caveat is that these theories (or explanations) offer a starting point for discussion and exploration into criminal behavior if members of the criminal justice system wish to pursue that line of study.

Since there are a number of theories offered and little time to cover them all in the Introduction to Criminal Justice course format, there needs to be a simple but somewhat broad acknowledgment of the theories that exist. Therefore, grouping the theories into three categories—biological, psychological, and sociological—is a good place to start. The following are suggested contents of the three categories that could facilitate teaching and discussion.

Biological

Within the realm of biological theories, one might indicate that there are three main bodies of thought. They are:

1. Abnormal physical structure (for example, Lombroso believed certain physical characteristics were associated with criminality or Sheldon believed body types could be related to crime).
2. Hereditary (an inheritance of certain physical traits, such as the X chromosome theory, and behavioral characteristics that lead to crime).
3. Biochemical (focuses upon biochemical disturbances and glandular malfunctions for inducing criminal acts).

Psychological

From the psychological perspective, one could advocate that there are three main explanations:

1. Psychoanalytical (for example, Freud's belief that criminal behavior was the result of an inadequately developed ego).
2. Cognitive development (inadequate moral development during childhood).
3. Social learning (criminals learn their behavior by modeling after behaviors of others who are criminal).

Sociological

This area can be perceived by some to be the most difficult to teach because there are a variety of theories, and it is impossible to discuss them all. Therefore, it is suggested that the following theories are among the more popular and best to discuss in such a short period:

1. Differential association (Sutherland believed that socialization with criminals produced criminality dependent upon frequency, duration, priority, and intensity).
2. Anomie (Merton believed that criminality is the result of one's adaptation of goal attainment [cultural goals] and the means [socially approved] used to achieve these goals. Five modes of adaptation include conformity ++, innovation +–, ritualism –+, retreatism ––, and rebellion +– and –+).
3. Labeling (Lemert's concept of social definitions).
4. Social control (Hirschi believed that an individual who becomes bonded or attached to the norms and values of society will not commit crime—dimensions include attachment, commitment, belief, and involvement).
5. Conflict (Marxist belief focuses on the people who have the political power to define crime for the rest of society).

To this point, those completely unfamiliar with the full content of a criminology course might think that this is a considerable amount of information, and it is. Imagine trying to teach all this in what usually is no more than a couple of class meetings. However, someone familiar with such a course recognizes that, at best, this information just skims the surface, but that is really all that is necessary for an introduction to criminal justice course. Still, it is far from acceptable for an introduction to criminology course, and it does not do justice to the full content of criminology.

INTRODUCTION TO CRIMINOLOGY

Although some of the following information will be repetitive, it is necessary to repeat some information to properly provide a suggested content of a criminology course as well as establish the main elements of criminology. Again, this material may be taught differently by instructors and might follow a different order or separation in an introductory textbook. However, the content itself does not change from one introductory course to another. In teaching this material, it is often easier to divide it into three sections, schools of thought, sociological criminology, and radical/contemporary criminology. That is the approach taken here, and we will begin with schools of thought.

SCHOOLS OF THOUGHT

As with most beginning sections, it is often customary to establish the foundations and bases for the remainder of the section. To accomplish this task, this section is divided into three parts: criminological foundations, the classical school, and the positive school.

Criminological Foundations

Criminological foundations can be viewed as the introduction to crime and criminality. Questions such as What is crime? Where does it come from? Why does it occur? and Is it truly a problem? can set the stage for the all the contents of criminology since one of its main goals is to attempt to provide answers. Furthermore, here is where defining criminology (which we will forego since that was accomplished in Chapter 2) and what criminologists do (which will be explored later in the text) can also be examined. This section may then be concluded with discussions of theory and the role of criminal law and the summation that there is no one way of viewing criminal behavior, which becomes extremely evident as the course continues. In all, this first part simply sets the table for the main entries, beginning with the foundation of criminology, the classical school.

Classical School

The classical school of thought is best examined in four parts. It can begin with a brief introduction of the classical school and the identification of the five main points noted in Chapter 1 (a social contract, free will, seek pleasure and avoid pain, punishment as a deterrent to crime, and identical punishment for identical crime).

The second part can involve what has been recognized as the preclassical school of thought. It is here that Cesare Beccaria and a main contemporary, Jeremy Bentham, are introduced. With respect to Beccaria, his essay *On Crimes and Punishment* (1963) is a great place to start. On punishment, Beccaria believed that the criminal penalty should inflict just enough pain to exceed the advantage that may have been gained had the crime been successful and that there should be a certainty of punishment. On crime and punishment, it was his contention that there is a proper proportion between the crime committed and the punishment meted out. In short, Beccaria was more concerned with encouraging reforms in the creation and application of criminal law than the determination of what caused criminal behavior.

Bentham's belief was that the purpose of law was to produce and support the complete happiness of the community. His take on punishment was that it should prevent crime, convince individuals to consider committing a lesser crime to ensure that no more force than necessary was applied, and to prevent crime cheaply. His famous statement was: "Let the punishment fit the crime." In short, the preclassical approach was deterrence of crime.

Part three might look at what has been referred to as the neoclassical (more popularly referred to as the statistical school). Here one would discuss how this school's views centered around the beliefs that there were many causes of crime such as circumstance, poverty, and population. Its main contributor was a Belgian mathematician, Quetelet, who has been identified as the first person to use objective mathematical techniques to investigate the influence of social factors on the propensity to commit crime. Some factors he studied included age, gender, season, climate, heterogeneity, professions, education, poverty, and alcohol. Quetelet's findings suggested that the greater the propensity, the greater the chances of the individual committing the crime.

Finally, the last part of this section is regarded as contemporary thought. For this, discussion focuses on the resurgence of the classical school of thought and notes that despite its strong presence in criminology today, it appears to have had little influence on criminological thought as a whole.

Positive School

The last topic under schools of thought is the positive school. This topic is best divided into three parts: introduction, biological, and psychological.

As part of the introduction, as with the classical school, one is advised to identify the main view of the positive school and its five major tenets (denial of free-will concept, multiple causes, causes are biological and environmental, use of scientific methods to look at causes, and actions toward the criminal to correct his problem). The focus of the positive school might also provide a brief acknowledgment of the types of early positivists, such as the biocriminologists who studied the shape of the head and body; physiognomists, who studied facial features; and phrenologists, who studied the shape of the skull and bumps on the head. This part usually concludes with an introduction to the "Holy Three": Lombroso, Ferri, and Garofalo.

The second area of the positive school encompasses the biological theories. Within the realm of these theories, a division into five categories is appropriate: physical, hereditary, body type, genetics, and other. Beginning with the physical theories, Lombroso is formally introduced. The underlying theme of his theory is that there is a positive correlation between physiques and crime. It is here where discussion of his theory can be more fully explored (recall that his theory identified four types of criminals: born, atavistic, insane, and others). As previously stated, while his theories are regarded more as historical curiosities and are scientifically unprovable, he was not alone in his beliefs.

To complete the discussion of the physical theories, three of Lombroso's contemporaries are often introduced: Goring, Garofalo, and Ferri. Goring was interested in the biometric method of study, applying statistical tests to the study of human characteristics, especially what he coined as "defective intelligence." It was his belief that criminal behavior was inherited and thus, regulating or controlling families displaying certain traits—such as feeblemindedness, epilepsy, and insanity—would limit criminal behavior. In contrast, Garofalo was more interested in criminal behavior as a psychic or moral anomaly. His belief was that an individual's lack of compassion and altruism—which led to criminal behavior—was organically linked. Finally, Ferri believed that delinquency and crime were linked to biological, social, and organic factors.

The second category, heredity, involves the study of families and criminality. The main theorists usually introduced in this section are Dugdale and Estabrook, who studied the Juke family tree, finding a number of criminals and delinquent offenders, and Goddard, who studied the Kallikak family, finding many criminal types. The assumption was that criminality breeds criminality. While the findings were taken seriously at the time, today's understanding of heredity and criminality eliminates the idea that crime is inbred.

Several individuals advocated the body-type theories. Kretschmer was one of the first criminologists to link body type (physique) with criminality. He identified individuals who committed less serious crimes as cyclothymites—soft-skinned with little muscle. They were also labeled as kindhearted, spontaneous, and lacking sophistication. Individuals who committed more serious crimes—schizothymites—were tall and flat or wide, muscular, and strong. They were characterized as having strong reactions and being apathetic.

A second contributor to the body-type theories was Sheldon, who claimed that there was a relationship between biological type and temperament. His three groupings included mesomorphs—well-developed, athletic, active, aggressive, and sometimes violent individuals; endomorphs—heavily built, slow moving, and lethargic individuals; and ectomorphs—tall, thin, less social, and more intellectual beings.

The third members of this group were Glueck and Glueck, who used Sheldon's theory to show that mesomorphs were disproportionately criminal. Finally, the radical of the group, McCandless, found that no relationship existed. Ultimately, the physical theories gave way to the genetic theories.

Genetic theories centered around biocriminological and sociobiological assumptions. The main genetic theorist was C. Ray Jeffery, who believed that genetics was partly to blame for criminal behavior. He postulated that genetic-code (X) environment equaled brain-code (X) environment, which equaled behavior. Within the genetic theories are the XYY chromosomal controversy, where the norm is males who are 46XY and females who are 46XX. Males discovered to be 47XYY were disproportionately inclined to commit criminal behavior; twin studies, where it was claimed that identical twins were more often likely to share criminal behaviors than fraternal twins; and adoptive studies, which indicated that if a father was criminal, the adoptive child tended to be criminal, too. For obvious reasons, genetic theories gained very little credence in criminological thought.

A relatively new field of endeavor with respect to biological theories should not go unnoticed and can be grouped as "other." It includes biochemical factors, such as vitamin and mineral deficiency, hypoglycemia, testosterone, and allergies as influencing criminality and neurophysiological conditions, such as brain dysfunction and tumors.

It should be noted that of all the biological theories, it is perhaps the last category (other) that has some potential in today's criminological field, particularly the biochemical factors (for example, the acceptance of PMS as a legitimate chemical imbalance that can affect a woman's behavior). However, as a whole, there is very little use for biological theory in today's criminological studies.

The last set of theories revealable under the positive school are those that fall under the psychological umbrella. As with the biological theories, the psychological theories can also be subdivided into four categories: personality, psychoanalytical, latent delinquency, and other.

Beginning with personality, the main theorist is Maudsley, who believed that insanity and criminal behavior were strongly linked. His contention was that crime was an outlet for unsound tendencies without which the individual would go insane and that it was hereditary. Today, insanity is not believed to be inherited, nor does it completely excuse a person from being punished or treated for the criminal behavior.

Probably the best known psychological theorist was Sigmund Freud and his psychoanalytical contributions. Freud believed that there existed a mental conflict that was a result of incompatible elements of the personality, and crime was the result of repressed personality experiences. His central argument was that delinquency and criminal behavior resulted from a failure of effective personal controls due to faulty early training or parental neglect.

Alternately, Freud believed that crime or delinquency was symptomatic of problems in coping with a basic issue of adjustment. Ultimately, Freud blamed sexual guilt retained from one's childhood Oedipus complex as a link to criminality. Today, even in psychological circles, Freud's theories garner little respect.

A third theory examinable under psychological theories is Aichorn's Latent Delinquency theory. Aichorn argued that problems experienced in the first few years of life make it impossible for the child to control impulses that can linger into adulthood as a type of aggrandizing infant who displays a pleasure orientation. The latent delinquent is characterized by seeking immediate gratification, considering personal needs satisfaction as more important than relating to others, and satisfying instinctive urges without consideration of right and wrong.

A last category of psychological theories might best be described as "other." It includes neurotic, psychotic, and psychobiological explanations. This section is best completed with a summation of psychological thought and a critique of psychological theories.

By completing the psychological theories, the discussion of the schools of thought is usually complete. This whole area of thought could be summarized as good potential for debate but limited in its applicable nature. Obviously there must be other means of explaining criminality. This is where sociological criminology is introduced.

SOCIOLOGICAL CRIMINOLOGY

For many instructors and students of criminology, this next section might best be considered the "heart and soul" of criminological thought. It is within this area that a majority of the criminological theories are generally introduced. Because of the number of theories and their different approaches and foci, this section may also be divided into major subdivisions. For this book's purpose, there are four: social process, social structure, social reaction, and social control. Each subdivision consists of a variety of theories that might be provided in a different order than what is offered here. However, this order does appear to be relatively common.

Social Process

Beginning with the social-process theories, six theories are commonly found for which their consistent theme is intimacy with criminal peers breeds criminality. Again, while the order of the discussion of these theories may vary, this one begins with what is considered the foundation of social-process theory, the theory of cultural deviance.

Cultural deviance was the product of Shaw and McKay's ecology of crime theory. This theory's general view was that criminal behavior is an expression of conformity to lower-class cultural values and traditions. Shaw and McKay attempted to explain crime and delinquency as a product of transition or change in the urban environment. They contended that transitional communities manifest social disorganization and maintain conflicting values and social systems. Shaw and McKay determined that environment strongly influenced criminal behavior. To support their theory, they offered what became recognized as the concentric circle theory, which takes the city of Chicago and divides it into five zones (starting with the innermost circle and moving away: I–Central Business District, II–Area in Transition, III–Working Men's Homes, IV–Residential District, and V–Commuter Zone). According to Shaw and McKay, the highest crime was in zone II, the area in transition. With all theories, there are strengths and weaknesses. The strengths of this theory are that it identifies why crime rates are highest in slum areas and points out the factors that produce crime. Its weaknesses are that it does not answer the following questions: Why does middle-class crime occur? Why are some youths insulated from a delinquent career? and What causes gang members to forego criminality as adults? Overall, this theory seemed to create more questions than it answered.

The next potential social-process theory one can explain is Sellin's culture conflict. The two main assumptions of this theory are:

1. Criminal law is an expression of the rules of the dominant culture; therefore, a clash may result between middle-class rules and splinter groups, such as ethnic and racial minorities who maintain their own set of conduct norms.
2. Obedience to the norms of their lower-class culture puts people in conflict with the norms of the dominant culture.

This theory is best summarized through its strengths (identifies the aspects of lower-class life that produce street crime and adds the idea of culture conflict to Shaw and McKay's theory) and weaknesses (it ignores middle-class crime completely and does not provide an adequate means of testing its theoretical premises).

Differential association, the third possible social-process theory, was posited by Sutherland. It is based on the laws of learning and includes the concept of symbolic interactionism. The basic focus is on social relations—the frequency, intensity, and meaningfulness of association rather than on the individual's qualities or traits or on the external world of concrete and visible events. Sutherland's major premise was that people learn to commit crime from their exposure to antisocial definitions; in particular, individuals will respond to the cultural standards of his or her associates, especially the intimate ones.

As with the previous theories, Sutherland's theory has its strengths and weakness, too. Its strengths include: explaining the onset of criminality, the presence of crime in all elements of social structure, and why some people in high-crime areas refrain from criminality. An additional strength is that it can apply to both juveniles and adults.

The theory's weaknesses include no answers to: Where do antisocial definitions originate? and How can we measure antisocial definitions or prove that someone has been exposed to an excess of them? The theory also fails to explain illogical acts of violence and destruction and offers no discussion as to how to adequately test the theory.

The discussion of differential association might then be followed with a brief look at the theory of differential anticipation. The main contributor of this theory was Glaser, whose major premise was that people commit crimes whenever and wherever expectations of gain from the criminal act exceed the expected losses with respect to social bonds. The strength of this theory is that it combines principles of social bond, differential association, and classical thought. However, its weaknesses are that it has not been subjected to extensive empirical testing, and it does not explain why expectations and crime rates vary.

A fifth social-process theory, and the last of the "differential" theories,[2] is Akers's differential reinforcement. Akers's major premise was that criminal behavior depends on the person's experiences, with rewards for conventional behaviors and punishments for deviant ones. The bottom line was that being rewarded for deviance only leads to more crime. While limited, the strengths of this theory are that it adds learning-theory principles to differential association, and it links sociological and psychological principles. The weaknesses of this theory are that it fails to explain (a) why those rewarded for conventional behavior will commit crimes and (b) why some delinquent youths do not become adult criminals despite their having been rewarded for criminal behavior.

[2.]   Actually it is the last of the differential theories that I place under the social-process heading. There is another differential theory that is introduced in the next section.

The last of the social-process theories available for discussion is learning theory, whose beginnings are attributed to Tarde's Theory of Imitation. Tarde noted that:

1. Individuals in close and intimate contact with one another imitate each other's behaviors.
2. Imitation spreads from the top down.
3. New acts and behaviors are superimposed on old ones and subsequently act to reinforce or to discourage previous customs (what he referred to as the Law of Insertion).

Tarde's theory is built upon by Bandura's social-learning theory, which claims that people learn to be aggressive and violent through life experiences. According to Bandura, aggressive acts are often the result of modeling. He identified three principle sources or models: family members, environmental experiences, and the mass media. (At this point, particularly in the classroom setting, it is often appropriate to discuss violent acts that center around the question, What triggers them? Some possible responses are the media, physical and mental abuse, and learned traits.) Bandura's theory can be concluded by looking at the four factors he attributes to producing violent and aggressive behavior: an event that heightens arousal, aggressive skills, expected outcomes, and consistency of behavior with values.

Note that strengths and weaknesses of this theory are not discussed because the jury is still out as to the merits of this theory. On the whole, social-process theories have led to many discussions as to whether criminal behavior is learned. Yet there are those who would argue that it is one's relationship to the social structure that leads to criminality.

Social Structure

A second group of theories one might focus on are those that follow the idea that criminality is the result of social structure. Five theories are identified and offered in this section: anomie, strain, delinquent boys, differential opportunity, and focal concern. It is easiest to begin with anomie, which might well be considered the basis for the remaining theories in this section.

Before the theory of anomie can be explained, the term *anomie* must be defined. What is meant by anomie is lawlessness that occurs when an individual no longer identifies with normative standards of conduct. Although Durkheim is credited with being the first to use the term in association with criminal behavior, Merton was the first person to incorporate it into a theory.

The root of anomie is *anomic stress,* which Merton described as the product of cultural values that counterpose a more or less common set of culturally defined goals that can be reached through socially accepted means. Based on this theory, criminal behavior is the result of an individual's inability to reach those goals through the approved means. The key to Merton's theory is adaptation, for which Merton supplied a typology of modes for adaptation (See Figure 3–1). Note that anomie aides in explaining the existence of high crime areas and the predominance of delinquent and criminal behavior among particular social and ethnic

Mode	Goals	Means	Behavior
Conformity	+	+	Stability
Innovation	+	–	Criminal
Ritualism	–	+	
Retreatism	–	–	Drugs, alcohol
Rebellion	+/–	+/–	

+ indicates acceptance of the goals and/or means
– indicates denial of goals and/or means

Figure 3–1.   Merton's Typology of Modes for Adaptation

groups. Yet while it manages to explain crime rates, it does not help explain particular behaviors. It is also noted that this theory led to advances in subcultural[3] explanations of delinquency (differential opportunity and delinquent boys).

The follow-up to anomie is *strain theory*, which focuses on an inability to reach higher goals or values because of one's economic placement in society. The prominent theorist in the development of strain theory was Emile Durkheim, a preeminent sociologist and criminologist. His beliefs included that crime:

- Is normal and necessary behavior,
- Is inevitable and linked to the differences within society,
- Can be useful, and even occasionally considered healthy, because the existence of crime implies that there is a way for social change and that social structure is not rigid or inflexible, and
- Calls attention to society's ills.

Durkheim is credited with coining the phrase "altruistic criminal," an individual who is offended by society's rules and seeks social change and an improved moral climate through his or her actions. He was also the first to consider that anomie or anomic stress was a cause of strain.

Returning to the extensions of anomie theory with delinquent boys theory—which was introduced by Cohen in his 1955 text *Delinquent Boys: The Culture of the Gang*—is required. The key points to Cohen's theory were that delinquency is due to status frustration, an inability to achieve success in a legitimate manner; that delinquency is a function of the social and economic limitations suffered by less fortunate individuals; and that the lower-class youth commits crime because he is unable to meet the standards of the middle class.

---

3. This refers to groups of persons who share similar ideas and values coming together for support, defense, and to fulfill mutual needs.

Cohen identified three types of behavior: corner boy, college boy, and delinquent boy. The most attention is paid to the delinquent boy, who adopts norms and principles directly opposite those of middle-class society. To fulfill this role, the youth joins a gang where activities are described as nonutilitarian, malicious, negativistic, versatile, short-run hedonistic, and autonomous (group peer pressure only). This theory is best concluded by noting the problems associated with it, such as little empirical support and assumptions that lower-class youths really care what the middle class thinks or really want what the middle class wants.

The other extension of anomie theory is differential opportunity, a theory introduced by Cloward and Ohlin in their 1960 text, *Delinquency and Opportunity*. The aim of this theory was to try and explain how delinquent male subcultures arise and persist in the lower-class areas of large urban cities. Their theory is based on the premise that the opportunities for lower-class youths to reach the American dream (education, wealth, status) are blocked, causing them to resort to illegitimate means. Cloward and Ohlin observed that as an alternative to reaching the American dream, satisfaction is gained by adapting to one of three subcultures (gangs): the criminal gang, which is the training ground for adult criminal activity; the conflict gang, where fighting and territorial protection is the norm; and the retreatist gang, which is content to search for kicks through alcohol, drugs, and sex. As with the other theories, it has its negatives and positives. However, it is one of the few theories that can be enhanced by relating it to today's gang problems.

The social-structure section may be completed with a short explanation of the focal concern theory which takes a cultural-deviance approach. The main view of focal concern theory is that criminality is a product of the values and attitudes ingrained in all elements of lower-class culture. Perpetuated by Miller, the major premise was that the individuals who follow the street rules of lower-class life find themselves in conflict with the dominant culture. The strength of this theory is that it more clearly identifies the aspects of lower-class culture that push people toward criminal behavior. Its weaknesses are that it does not provide empirical support for the existence of a lower-class culture, account for middle-class influence, or explain upper-class crime.

To conclude, the social-structure theories tend to have some relevancy for today's attempts to understand criminality. Still, one should be aware that these theories all focused on male youths who were drawn to gangs. This places serious limitations on the utility of these theories for current explanations of youth criminal behavior in or outside of a gang. Perhaps it is not so much social structure but rather one's reaction to society that leads to criminality.

Social Reaction

A third-phase possibility of sociological criminological thought involves two theories, labeling and commitment to conformity, both of which have been designated as social-reaction theories. To begin requires an overview of what social-reaction theorists have postulated. They begin by advising that it is impossible to understand criminality merely through the study of criminals; it must be viewed in its entire social context. Social-reaction theories argue that criminal behavior can only be understood in the context of how others react to it. This includes official reactions in which individuals and events are legally defined as criminal. It has been argued that criminal behavior is defined solely by the reactions that others have to it, creating what can be referred to as a "reactive" definition of crime.

Social-reaction theories can best be summarized as attempting to explain the occurrence of criminal behavior prior to the societal reaction on the basis of social disorganization, and additional occurrences of criminal behavior after the societal reaction are a result of socialization. This leads to the question, Is it the reaction of an individual or of a group that influences the behavior? The two theories assist in responding to this question.

The main social-reaction theory has been recognized as Lemert's labeling theory. The main assumptions of this theory are:

1. Two types of deviance exist: primary, where crimes are situationally induced, and secondary, which is the result of labels and sanctions occurring from primary deviance.
2. Individuals will enter into a career of law violations when they are labeled for their personalities around the labels, especially if done so by significant others.
3. Labeling has two effects: creating a stigma and effecting self-image.[4]
4. Labeled individuals view themselves as deviant and will commit increasing amounts of criminal behavior.

Like the other theories, labeling theory has its strengths and weaknesses. Its strengths include explanations of the role that society has in creating deviance and why some juvenile delinquents do not become adult criminals. It also helps develop the concept of career criminal. The weaknesses are that it does not explain the reason the crime was originally committed, and it places too much emphasis on society's role.

To complement the theory of labeling, there is Briar and Piliavan's commitment to conformity theory. This theory's main assumption was that short-term stimuli that influence behavior are controlled by the individual's commitment to conventional society. This commitment is believed to help resist temptations. The positive aspects of this theory is that it can help explain both middle- and lower-class criminality and can

---

4. To better illustrate this point in my classes, I have a 1987 Broom Hilda cartoon that I share with students. The cartoon shows the main character in one panel chasing a car, barking like a dog. In the last panel, she is shown walking away and saying, "When you've been called a dog often enough, it does things to your psyche!!" (Tribune Media Services, Inc., 8/12/1987)

show how control is manifested over the middle class not to commit crime. The negative side of this theory is that it fails to explain variations in crime and crime rates and why some children develop commitments and others do not.

Completing the discussion of commitment to conformity theory brings about the conclusion for social-reaction theories. At this point, a brief summary of these theories suggests that one may commit criminal behavior in response to how society reacts, but they do not offer why the behavior occurs in the first place or, for that matter, why many individuals do not commit crime. Perhaps there are certain social controls that help limit this behavior.

Social Control

The last section that will be brought forth under sociological criminology is that which introduces the social-control theories. These theories start with an assumption that human nature is the motivator for criminal behavior. It is believed that if some type of controls did not exist, individuals would naturally commit crimes.

The first of the self-described control theorists, Reiss, argued that the failure of personal controls (the inability to refrain from meeting personal needs in ways that conflict with society's norms and rules) leads to criminality. However, he failed to consider the effect of family, environment, and community controls on an individual's behavior. Despite the obvious flaws in his thinking, Reiss's assumptions made way for three social-control theories: drift, containment, and social bond.

The drift (sometimes called neutralization) theory was proposed by Matza and Sykes. Their main assumption was that youths learn ways to neutralize society's moral constraints and will periodically drift in and out of criminal behavior. They contended that delinquency is essentially an unrecognized extension of "defenses to crimes" in a form of justifications. In other words, criminal behavior can be rationalized by the offender but not by the legal system or society. These rationalizations can precede or follow criminal behavior and are said to serve to protect the individual from self-blame and blame of others after the act. Matza and Sykes identified five ways that delinquents could rationalize or neutralize their actions:

1. Denial of responsibility—which extends beyond the concept of accident and implies that the deviant act resulted from forces beyond the individual's control;
2. Denial of injury—despite being unlawful behavior, the individual does not feel that the behavior really harmed anyone;
3. Denial of victim—again, despite being unlawful, the belief is that the victim deserved the action taken against him or her and that the act was actually a form of punishment rather than injurious;
4. Condemnation of the condemners—this focuses attention from the deviant act to those who have condemned it; and
5. Appeal to higher loyalties—here legal norms are replaced by a loyalty to other norms.

The strengths of the drift theory include explanations as to why many delinquents do not become adult criminals and why youthful law violators can participate in conventional behavior. The theory's weaknesses are that it fails to show whether neutralization occurs before or after the criminal behavior, explain why some youths drift and others do not, and explain self-destructive acts like alcohol and drug usage.

Another of the social-control theories is referred to as the containment theory. The main theorist, Reckless, claimed that each person has inner and outer controls that push toward conformity or pull toward criminality. He further contended that society produces these pushes and pulls, which can be counteracted by internal and external containments. Five elements are identified:

1. Inner containment—the individual's personality;
2. Outer containment—the constraints that society and social groups use;
3. Internal pushes—personal factors such as restlessness, discontent, and boredom;
4. External pressures—such as adverse living conditions; and
5. External pulls—such as deviant associates.

The strengths of this theory are that it brings together psycho- and sociological principles and can explain why some people are able to resist the strongest social pressures to commit crime. It has been criticized over the methodology used to support it.

The last of the social-control theories is Hirschi's social-bond (or control) theory. Its main assumption was that it is the person's bond to society that prevents him or her from participating in criminal behavior. Should the bond weaken, the individual feels free to commit crime. Hirschi identified four elements of a bond to conventional society: attachment, commitment, involvement, and belief. From a positive perspective, the social-bond theory explains the onset of criminality, applies to both middle- and lower-class crime, and explains its theoretical constructs in a manner that can be measured and empirically tested. From a negative perspective, it fails to explain the differences in crime rates, show whether a weak bond can be strengthened, and distinguish the importance of different elements of the social bond (which is more important—attachment or commitment, commitment or involvement, and so on?).

Overall, social-control theories do not afford us any better explanations, as a whole, than do any of the other theories offered under the rubric of sociological criminology. Although they do allow for serious discussion and possible application, they still leave many unanswered questions of applicability to adults and to whether these theories apply to today's juveniles, too, considering that most of these theories were developed in the 1950s and 1960s. This means that there must still be other possible explanations to explore, particularly theories with a more modern slant. Therefore, a last section of possible theories is provided.

RADICAL AND CONTEMPORARY CRIMINOLOGY

The last section of this chapter looks at what may be considered the newer attempts at explaining criminality, radical and contemporary theories. Despite sharing the same umbrella, each concept is discussed separately, beginning with radical criminology.

Unlike the schools of thought where application of law and punishment, biological, psychological, sociological factors, or in sociological criminology where individual and societal relationships are the mainstay for explaining criminal behavior, the radical criminological theories emphasize "society" as the major influence on criminal behavior because society's powerful control the nonpowerful. The essence of radical criminology is conflict theory.

Conflict theories attempt to identify society's power relations and draw attention to their role in promoting criminal behavior. Although conflict is viewed as an essential social process upon which society depends, group interests and their influence on legislation that arise from these conflicts are linked to criminal behavior. The conflict model espouses three themes:

1. The relativity of criminal definitions. Conflict theory says that every act defined as immoral, deviant, or criminal must be viewed as tentative at best and that it is always

subject to redefinition (depending on the group with the most power).

2. Control of institutions. Conflict theorists debate that there are three basic means to maintaining and enhancing society's interests: force, compromise, and the dominance of social institutions, such as law, church, schools, and government.

3. Law as an instrument of power. Viewed as an extremely potent weapon of social conflict, whoever has control over the laws retains powers.

Conflict theory views crime as the ability of those groups in power to protect themselves and their interests, thus leading those not in power toward criminal behavior. To date, four conflict theories have been offered: Marxist, group, social reality, and criminalization.

Radical Criminology

Better known as the social-conflict theory and considered the foundation of conflict theory, Marxist theory is where explaining radical criminology begins. The general views from Marxist theory are that:

- There is struggle between the proletariate (working class) and the bourgeoisie (money).
- Political and economic philosophy of dominant class influences all aspects of life.
- Society's structure(s) are unstable and could be changed through slow and evolving violence.

Two individuals credited with Marxist theory require introductions: Marx and Bonger. Although the theory is named after Marx, Bonger has been viewed as the earliest and best known of the conflict theorists. His six views might well be the foundation of conflict theory. Bonger had noted that:

- The abnormal element of crime is of social and biological origin.
- The response to crime is punishment—the application of penalties considered more severe than spontaneous moral condemnation.
- No act is naturally immoral or criminal.
- Crimes are antisocial acts harmful to those who have the power at their command to control society.
- In every society divided into ruling class and an inferior class, penal law serves the will of the former.
- Crime is a function of poverty.

Marx's view was that class biases are due to class division; where a capitalist society is made up of two classes—elite (bourgeoisie) and subordinates (proletariat)—conflict is inevitable. His solution was a classless society with the overthrowing of capitalistic society and adoption of a socialistic system as the keys.

Marxist theory pulls together the views of both Bonger and Marx, offering a different view of law and behavior than any of the other schools of thought or theories previously discussed. For example, the Marxist view of law and behavior is that individuals are not naturally inclined to be either criminal or non-criminal and that the inclination toward criminal behavior is a result of social circumstance (laws). These social circumstances are believed to encourage altruism (which inhibits criminality) and egoism (which encourages criminality). In examining Marxist theory, the underlying key seems to be law(s), which leads to discussing responses to the following five questions:

1. Are laws the product of political process? *Marxist theorists argue yes by noting who it is that influences them.*
2. Does class conflict produce law? *Marxist theorists tend to believe that this is the case.*

3. Does group conflict produce law? *A Marxist theorist would say that it is a product of multiple interests.*
4. Is there generally social consensus about laws? *A Marxist theorist would claim that there is not.*
5. Is a single dominant class or a number of relatively powerful, competing interest groups behind legislation and law enforcement? *The Marxist response would be yes, and is twofold: the ruling elite, owner capitalists, and those who own the ability to manufacture and produce or the working class simply because of its numerical advantage.*

In completing the examination of Marxist theory, a brief summation could center around the idea that according to this theory, the ruling elite have control that forces subordinates into criminal behavior. No discussion is complete without taking into consideration the criticisms of this theory, which include failing to look at the problems associated in establishing a socialistic society and the differential enforcement of the laws.

Because the remaining three conflict theories are fundamentally similar to Marxist theory, highlighting only the main points seems prudent at this juncture. Beginning with Vold, his group-conflict theory simply postulates that conflict between groups should be viewed as one of the principal and essential social processes upon which the continuing ongoing of society depends.

Quinney, whose theory is known as the social-reality theory, advocates that conflict is intertwined with power and that differential distribution of power produces conflict, which is rooted in the competition for power. Quinney offered six postulates for explaining conflict as social reality; they included:

1. The definition of crime—Crime is a definition of human conduct that is created by authorized agents in a politically organized society.
2. The formulation of criminal definition—Criminal definitions describe behaviors that conflict with the interests

of those segments of society having the power to shape public policy.

3. The application of criminal definition—Criminal definitions are applied by the segments of society that have the power to shape the enforcement and administration of criminal law.
4. The development of behavior patterns in relation to criminal definition—Behavior patterns are structured in segmentally organized society in relation to criminal definitions, and within this context persons engage in actions that have relative probabilities of being defined as criminal.
5. The construction of criminal conceptions—Conceptions of crime are constructed and diffused in the segments of society by various means of communication.
6. The social reality of crime—The social reality of crime is constructed by the formulation and application of criminal definitions and the construction of criminal conceptions.

Finally, there is Austin Turk's criminalization theory, whose main views center around:

- The conditions under which cultural and social differences between authorities and subjects will probably result in conflict,
- The conditions under which criminalization will probably occur in the course of conflict, and
- The conditions under which the degree of deprivation associated with becoming a criminal will probably be greater or lesser.

Completing this discussion on Turk also completes the discussion of radical criminology, which leads into the most recent approach to criminological theory grouped under the label *contemporary*.

Contemporary Criminology

Unlike all the previous main segments, in introducing this segment it is difficult to provide a synopsis of contemporary theories because it is still so new that there really is not a major theme that runs through them. Realistically, to date, contemporary theory is still trying to define itself and find its place in criminological thought. For the purpose at hand, note that there are not yet any theories to offer, only explorations of criminality previously ignored in criminological studies that could conceivably become theories. The two areas most identifiable for this segment are routine activity and female criminality.

The concept of routine theory was brought forth by Cohen and Felson, who believe that changes in routine activities of everyday life can lead to criminality. They contend that the structure of such activities influences criminal opportunity and therefore affects trends in a class of crimes, which they label as direct-contact predatory violations—illegal acts where an individual definitively and intentionally takes or damages the person or property of another. Their argument rests on the belief that structural changes in routine activity patterns can influence crime rates by affecting the convergence in space and time of the three minimal elements of direct-contact predatory violations: motivated offenders, suitable targets, and absence of capable guardians against a violation. Their ultimate conclusion is that criminality is a given.

The other area deserving attention is female criminality. Historically, women have been ignored in criminological thought. Although the reasons are obvious— their low rates of criminal and delinquent behavior, and most criminological theorists have been males—female criminality cannot be ignored. The early theoretical work that has been attributed to female criminality can be viewed as individualist—that is, focusing on the physiological, psychological, and inherent nature of women, which is believed to be universal. However, in exploring more recent endeavors to explain female criminality, some underlying themes are discovered that include: the woman's perversion of or rebellion against their natural roles; their work-related roles in society as being more service oriented; linking sexuality, which is seen as the root of female behavior and the problem with criminal behavior; that criminality may be a response to the need for equality or an attempt to become less feminine and more masculine; and that criminal behavior is biologically, psychologically, and sociologically influenced.

Since it is a new and growing area, this view remains extremely flexible and open for new information. It can be concluded with the thought, What should be the focus of current criminologists? A consistent response or inquiry to this is the environment, particularly poverty, which is often touted as a reason for crime. In response, the following is offered.

It is suggested that among all the possible environmental factors, poverty is the one that has been most attributed to crime and criminal behavior. Therefore, the most obvious question is, Does poverty cause crime? Before an answer can be sought, it helps to know what is meant by poverty. Simply put, poverty refers to the inability to procure or meet an economically defined level of income that allows for minimal survival and well-being. For example, at the time of this writing, the poverty level in the United States was below $15,600 for a family of four.[5] A key component of poverty seems to be unemployment. Those few studies that have been attempted examined either poverty or unemployment.[6] The results are ambiguous at best.

A curious point is knowing why these studies are so inconsistent. One plausible explanation is that most of these studies may be methodologically flawed because of terminology. Consider that while poverty is more readily recognized, researchers

---

[5.] This number was cited in a December 23, 1996, issue of *U.S. News and World Report* in a brief piece entitled "The Poorest Among Us" (p. 18).

[6.] The studies I mention here were conducted by Guerry, Quetelet, Glaser, and Rice, and Danser and Laub.

of this phenomenon as it relates to crime also need to contemplate these terms: economic inequality and relative deprivation.

Because materialism is a strong part of our American culture, criminologists should compare the level of those who have little in the way of material belongings to the level of others in society, thus recognizing economic inequality. Relative deprivation is the result of the economic inequality combined with resentment and a sense of injustice among those who have the least in society. This relative deprivation could conceivably have greater influence on criminality than poverty. With the addition of these terms to the mix, it opens up a whole new approach to whether poverty is really a true influence on crime.

At this point two things should be clear, that (a) teaching criminology requires an extensive knowledge of theory, research, and policy, and (b) as a field of study, criminology offers a broad array of possibilities for explaining criminal behavior. In either case, simply knowing criminological thought is not enough to truly understand criminal behavior. Obviously there is more to it than meets the eye. Perhaps that is where criminal justice comes in.

CONCLUSION

This chapter has provided a plethora of information. Its intent was to describe the content of a complete introductory criminology course and the mainstays of criminological thought within the space of a single chapter. In doing so, the main content revolves around three primary divisions: schools of thought, sociological theories, and radical and contemporary theories. Obviously there is much more depth and breadth possible, which is why there are complete introductory textbooks as well as upper-level courses that spend more time in deeper examination and study of criminological theory. However, the goal here was to suggest what the main components, concepts, and ideas of criminology are as they might appear in an introductory class in criminal justice, criminology, or related textbooks. Furthermore, despite its limitations, the contents of this chapter are substantial enough to allow comparisons, contrast, and the intertwining of criminology and criminal justice. Still, it is obvious that this cannot occur until you are subjected to a similar rendering of the content of criminal justice from similar perspectives as given in this chapter on criminology.

FOR THE CRITICAL THINKER

1. Based on the content of this chapter, how difficult does it appear to be able to explain or teach about the contents of criminology?
2. You have been asked to give a brief summary of what constitutes criminology. What would be your main points? How might you incorporate the social focus aspect of criminology?
3. Considering the three main divisions of criminology as offered in this chapter, which would you suggest as being the most relevant to explaining criminality in today's society? Why?
4. Why do you think that the bulk of social criminological thought is directed toward juvenile criminality? How difficult would it be to apply most of these theories to adult criminality?
5. In light of what has been offered as "criminology," what is missing? What directions should modern and future criminologists take toward expanding the theoretical base?

Criminal Justice

4

Since the mid-1970s, the number of criminal justice programs has grown substantially. Depending on which source you accept, there are easily over 1000 university and college programs that offer some form of degree plan in criminal justice. It is safe to assume, without a doubt, that the beginning course in almost every one of these programs is introduction to criminal justice. The result of its popularity has been the writing and publishing of numerous textbooks.[1] As with introductory criminology textbooks, one might observe in reviewing several introductory criminal justice textbooks, that the content is similar; just the order and how it is displayed tends to differ. Therefore, it is conceivable that while each instructor will have a different style of presentation, the material presented will generally be consistent.

---

[1] If you are curious, examine the bibliography, where you should be able to identify at least 15 introductory CJ textbooks.

In the previous chapter you were provided with what are considered the basic topics of criminology for both introduction to criminal justice and introduction to criminology courses. Chapter 3 also provided what are believed to be the bases of the study of criminology. This chapter will follow suit by establishing what is believed to be the foundations of criminal justice as a discipline and the standard content matter that is consistent with an introduction to criminal justice course. This is accomplished by examining criminal justice in five sections: introduction, police, courts, corrections, and juvenile justice. Again, it should be considered that while individual instructors will spend more time on some areas over others, ultimately all the basic information offered should be examined.

INTRODUCTION

Prior to being able to fully discuss the criminal justice system's (CJS) components or subsystems, it is important to understand what it is meant by criminal justice and its primary elements. Therefore, the first step is to establish the important underlying aspects of criminal justice by way of an introductory section that can be subdivided into four areas: foundations, perspectives, crime, and criminal law.

Foundations

As with any topic or in an introductory course, it is best to begin with defining the main concept—in this case, criminal justice. Having done this in an earlier chapter, it will not be done so here, but in a course, this would be the place to examine the definitions. Furthermore, in a course, one could begin by asking students to try to define criminal justice—or at least attempt to obtain their perceptions of what is meant by criminal justice before providing the more formal definitions. This can be followed by a brief introduction of the term *criminology*. An understanding of the difference between the two is imperative and helps enlighten students as to what it is they are and are not going to be studying (if you need to refresh your memory as to the definition used, refer back to Chapter 2). With this distinction made clear, we can now move forward.

Systems/Subsystems

Once a person understands the concept of criminal justice through definition, the next step is to understand why one studies criminal justice. It can be suggested that its study has comparative value; that it can assist in explaining, predicting, identifying, and influencing operations, policies, and so on of the criminal justice system and its components; that ultimately it can provide background and knowledge for individuals who work within the system, are seeking employment in the system, or who simply wish to better understand the system.[2] The emphasis is placed on understanding the system because, as noted earlier, criminal justice is both a social concept recognized as the criminal justice system and a field of study. Therefore, the next step is to introduce the concept of systems.

An inquiry of individuals, especially students, as to what they consider a system can offer interesting results. It would seem that many might recognize a system but find it difficult to define. Therefore, the following definition, as it applies to criminal justice, can be offered:

> A system is a set of interrelated parts working independently or jointly toward a specific objective or goal within a complex environment. The criminal justice system (CJS) is an open system comprising three subsystems: police, courts, and corrections. (See Figure 4–1 as a simple illustrative example.)

[2.] It has been my experience that despite the large number of students majoring in criminal justice, there is often an equal or greater number who take an introductory CJ course as an elective with some hopes of gaining a better understanding of a system that has so much influence on how we live.

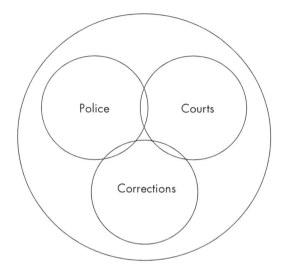

Figure 4–1. The Criminal Justice System

This definition is reinforced by noting that the CJS consists of lawmaking bodies as well as local, state, and federal agencies charged with enforcing the law and punishing those who are violators. Overall, the CJS consists of three main components or subsystems, each of which will be examined later in the text. Furthermore, it should also be noted that it is common for courses and textbooks devoted to a single component or subsystem to exist and be offered as part of a criminal justice curriculum. Yet to understand the system, one must have some idea of its history.

History

Since the history of criminal justice could be a course of its own (and is in some schools), only a brief history will be provided here. The study of criminal justice dates back to the mid-18th century. Beginning in 1919, we have seen the formation of several entities that conducted research dealing with criminal justice policy. Examples include the Chicago Crime Commission (1919), Wickersham Commission (1931), President's Commission on

Law Enforcement and Administration of Justice (1967), and National Advisory Commission on Criminal Justice Standards and Goals (1973). The history of criminal justice finds that it is an interdisciplinary field (components of political science, economics, sociology, psychology, public administration, et cetera) that focuses on the nature of crime in society and analyzes the formal processes and agencies of crime control. Furthermore, the establishment of the system, the laws, policies, processes, functions, and so on involve all three branches of government:

1. *Legislature*—Primary responsibility is to define criminal behavior and establish penalties. It also passes laws pertaining to criminal procedures—laws of arrest, search and seizure, and so forth.
2. *Judiciary*—Primary responsibility is to conduct trials and sentence the guilty, interpret the law, and weigh its constitutionality.
3. *Executive*—Plans programs, appoints personnel, and exercises administrative responsibility for criminal justice agencies.

Therefore, it is safe to say that the CJS is broad in scope and nature and reflects the interrelationships among all entities involved with controlling crime, in particular, the three main components.

Components

During the establishment of criminal justice as a system, its three main components have been identified. At this point, a brief explanation of each subsystem's role seems appropriate.

Police: Beginning with the police subsystem, it is suggested that its primary concern is with maintaining order and enforcing the criminal law. Three levels—federal, state, and local—exist. It is estimated that over 14,000 police agencies are part of this subsystem.

Courts: The courts determine criminal responsibility and are expected to convict the guilty and protect the innocent. Like the police subsystem, the court subsystem also consists of three levels—federal, state, and local—and each is divided into three primary divisions—lower courts, superior (trial) courts, and supreme (appeals) courts. The prosecution and defense, as well as probation, is found within this subsystem.

Corrections: The corrections subsystem is charged with supervising the convicted through incarceration, probation, and parole. There are three levels of this subsystem, too. It is often the least funded yet often the most demanded upon component of the system (at least in terms of expectations for results in behavioral changes).

In concluding the discussion of the components, one should be made aware of the fifteen steps (See Table 4–1) associ-

Table 4–1. Steps in the Criminal Justice System's Process

Process/Step	Subsystem
(1) Initial contact	(P)
(2) Investigation	(P)
(3) Arrest	(P)
(4) Custody	(P)
(5) Complaint	(P/Ct)
(6) Preliminary and/or Grand Jury hearing	(Ct)
(7) Arraignment	(Ct)
(8) Bail/Detention	(Ct)
(9) Plea bargaining	(Ct)
(10) Adjudication/Trial	(Ct)
(11) Disposition/Sentencing	(Ct)
(12) Postconviction remedies/Appeals	(Ct)
(13) Incarceration	(Co)
(14) Release	(Co/Ct)
(15) Post-release	(Co)

P = Police   Ct = Courts   Co = Corrections

ated with the process of the criminal justice system. In examining each step, one can recognize and indicate which subsystem is most responsible for carrying out the step. At the conclusion of identifying all 15 steps, it is discovered that the court subsystem appears to have the most responsibility (in terms of number of steps attributed to it), but is often the least funded of the three systems.[3] From here, we can now focus on the system's goals and issues.

Goals and Issues

In studying the CJS, a very important aspect must not be forgotten: goals and issues. A basic problem that exists within the CJS is that it lacks a commonly agreed upon philosophy and set of goals. Each subsystem has its beliefs and philosophies; however, there are some commonalities. The more obvious common goals include: preventing crime, diverting offenders, deterring crime, controlling criminals, rehabilitation, and general protection of society. There are also some less tangible goals, such as fairness, efficiency, effectiveness, evaluation, and standard setting. This often leads to this question, What should be the goal(s) of the system and each component/subsystem?

As with the goals, there are a number of identifiable issues that can be reflected within each subsystem, but each may be more weighted in one subsystem over another. The issues often identified include:

- Victim's rights
- The inability to unify the system
- Financial problems
- The changing concepts of crime causation
- Recidivism and the failures of rehabilitation

[3.] For example, in 1992 the total amount of expenditures of the justice system, for all levels of government, was over $93 billion: $41 billion was spent for police protection, $21 billion on judicial and legal issues, and $31+ billion for corrections.

- The narrowing scope of social control
- The debate of civil liberties vs. crime control
- The system's inability to prevent and control crime.

Obviously these issues can lead to commentary and debate as to which is the most critical and least critical, and to identifying any others. However, while that will not be done here, it is strongly suggested for the classroom.

What to Do with a CJ Degree

Finally, understanding the foundations can be enhanced by understanding what an individual might do with a degree in criminal justice. Employment opportunities in policing, courts, corrections, academia, and research are possibilities that can be explored.

In sum, there are a number of topics that are related to setting the foundation or introducing criminal justice. Once these have been grasped, the next step is to examine the different perspectives of criminal justice.

Perspectives

As in most areas of study, there are always differing views or perspectives. The same can be said for criminal justice. There are six models or perspectives of interest, each providing a somewhat different way to approach criminal justice.

1. **Crime Control** (classical school)—The main concern of this model is with the protection of society through the control of actual or potential criminal offenders. It is believed that this can be accomplished through police protection, mandatory prison sentences, incapacitation, and the death penalty. Believers in the crime-control perspective lay claim to the views of swift and sure jus-

tice, opposing legal restrictions that control police actions, and have no faith in rehabilitation.

2. **Rehabilitative**—Purveyors of the rehabilitative perspective call for the treatment of offenders. They believe that people are at the mercy of social, economic, and interpersonal conditions and that criminals are victims of racism, poverty, lack of hope, alienation, and other social problems. The belief is that crime can be controlled by assisting individuals in obtaining their goals and coping with life situations.

3. **Due Process**—This perspective was very big in the 1960s and early 1970s. Basically, due process is concerned with legal fairness as prescribed by the Constitution—that is, fair and equitable treatment for those accused of a crime. Primary support for this view was aided by the U.S. Supreme Court landmark decisions in such cases as *Miranda, Mapp, Escobedo, In re Gault,* and *Gideon*.

4. **Nonintervention**—This perspective calls for limited involvement by the government. It promotes decriminalization, deinstitutionalization, and pretrial diversion.

5. **Justice**—A combination of liberal and conservative views, this perspective stresses crime control and punishment as well as fairness, equality, and strict control of discretion, treating offenders on the basis of current behavior. This model is tabbed as being what the CJS should reflect but somehow has not been able to.

6. **Radical**—This perspective views the CJS as a state-supported effort to control the powerless, placing more emphasis on concern of police misuse of power, discrimination, and discretion.

Obviously, examination of these models can lead to interesting debate and discussion. It also lends itself to introducing the next area, which is the reason why we even have differing perspectives and is a main link with criminology: crime.

Crime

The overriding reason for the CJS to even exist is because of crime. Therefore, this area becomes an extremely important part of understanding criminal justice. One can begin by trying to define what is meant by crime. It is advocated that one take a very simplistic approach: Crime is any action or failure to act as described within the penal code (criminal laws) of a state or the federal government.

To enhance, or perhaps even confuse, one's understanding of crime, there are three differing views:

- **Consensus**—A general agreement that crimes are behaviors that are essentially harmful to the majority of citizens and have been controlled or prohibited by the existing criminal law. It views criminal law as a set of rules that express the norms of society and has a social-control function that serves to restrain individuals who would take advantage of others for personal gain.
- **Interactionist**—The interactionist agrees that criminal law defines the actions constituting a crime but challenges the belief that the law represents the will of a majority of citizens. Instead, the interactionist views criminal law as being influenced by people who hold social power and use it to mold the law to reflect their interests.
- **Conflict**—Views criminal law as a means of protecting the power of the upper class at the expense of the poor. It is based on the premise that society is a collection of diverse groups who are in constant conflict where certain groups are able to assert their power and use the criminal law to advance their interests.

What these views allow is a demonstration that there is no consensus as to what is meant by crime. However, it has been argued that through integration of the three perspectives, a singular definition can arise: Crime is a violation of societal rules of behavior as interpreted and expressed by a criminal code created by people holding social and political power.[4] Agreement or disagreement with this definition and how it might apply to today's view of crime is definitely food for thought. It also makes it easier to look at what identifies some activity (or lack thereof) as a crime: the law.

Law

Because law is mentioned within the context of the previous material, and this introductory section concludes with an in-depth look at criminal law, at this juncture the choice is made to simply pose two questions: What is meant by criminal law? and What influences criminal law? Although the answers will become clear shortly, what about the way we keep track of crime? That is, what about all those statistics we always hear about?

Crime Statistics

Our society seems to put considerable interest and faith into numbers, in particular, all forms of statistics. This is especially true with respect to crime statistics. Therefore, it is necessary to review the concept, existence, and use of crime statistics. To meet this challenge, one might begin by asking and answering two questions: What are statistics? and What are crime statistics?

Statistics, simply put, are numbers assigned to an item, event, or activity in an effort to keep track of or measure them. Crime statistics are numbers assigned to events or activities associated with criminal behavior, such as arrests, convictions,

---

[4.] Unfortunately, I have used this example for many years and no longer know whether I actually came up with it or if it should be credited to another. Therefore, I do not claim it is my own idea but neither can I cite the proper authority.

or the number of occurrences of a particular crime (for example, murders in America for a given year).

Further understanding of crime statistics requires identifying the three main ways in which crime data is often reported:

1. As raw figures (actual numbers)(for example, in 1996 there were 200 murders in a given city);
2. As a percentage of change from previous years (for example, robberies decreased 3.6 percent in 1996 from 1995); and
3. As a rate per 100,000 people (for example, nationally, in 1993 there were 15.2 rapes reported per 100,000 people).

Where one finds these types of data is the next issue.

While there are a variety of sources of crime statistics, the best known and most used source is the *Uniform Crime Reports* (UCR), compiled and reported by the Federal Bureau of Investigation (FBI). Every month law enforcement agencies voluntarily report the number of offenses reported to their agency to the FBI. Since there are several hundred types of crimes varying from state to state, not all crimes can be included. Therefore, the UCR is primarily concerned with *index* crimes. These include: murder and nonnegligent manslaughter, forcible rape, robbery, aggravated assault, burglary, larceny, arson, and auto theft. They are reported even if there are no arrests, no recovery of property, and whether or not prosecution occurs.

Other data reported in the UCR are arrest rates, which include age, gender, and ethnicity/race of offender. Using the UCR we can examine a variety of crime trends (albeit tentatively) in the U.S.

Although the UCR provides us with a variety of crime data, there are flaws that must be acknowledged:

1. Reporting practices by the police,
2. Lack of reporting by victims,
3. Improper classification,

4. Downgrading charges/plea bargaining,
5. Under-/overreporting by police,
6. Political manipulation, and
7. Technical flaws.

These flaws have led to the question of the UCR's validity. Yet, the UCR still provides a starting point and some insight into patterns of crime such as ecological and geographical differences, gender differences, race and ethnicity, and age.

Due to the flaws and concerns with the overall validity of the UCR two alternative sources for crime statistics exist: National Crime Survey (Victimization Studies) and Self-Report Surveys. Furthermore, currently under development, and projected as the replacement to the UCRs, is the National Incident Based Reporting System (NIBRS), which will allow the reporting of a greater variety of crimes than previously capable in the UCRs.

Finally, the last area to consider within the realm of crime is the influence of criminology on criminal justice. Having already addressed this information in Chapter 2, it seems prudent to simply advise, if necessary, a return to that section for review. This takes us up to the last part of the introductory material: criminal law.

Criminal Law

As previously noted, crime is the central element of the criminal justice system. What constitutes a crime is that which is defined as such and recognized because of its existence within criminal law. Therefore, it is now necessary to examine what is criminal law.

It has been said that criminal law is the legal code that represents the influence of a number of sources attempting to control public behavior by defining what constitutes a crime. Rather than actually offer a standard definition, it has been suggested that criminal law is best recognized as consisting of four dimensions: politics, specificity, uniformity, and punishment.

Briefly, with respect to politics, criminal laws are a product of legislatures (which often are comprised of elected officials). These laws will often be the result of a partisan cause or the efforts of a lobbyist group. For example, the Mothers Against Drunk Drivers (MADD) have been a strong influence toward the increase in laws and punishments for driving while intoxicated or under the influence of alcohol or drugs.

Specificity refers to the fact that the law must normally be clear and direct as to what actions (or nonactions) are required to establish a crime. In the case of robbery, the law might read: "A person commits a robbery when he or she deprives or takes property of another from that person by force or threat of force." There is no doubt as to what is meant by a robbery.

Uniformity requires that the law be written and applied in a manner that constitutes equality among all members of society. That is, the law is not directed toward any one specific individual or group, or only applicable to certain regions of a state or the country.

Finally, in order for a criminal law to exist, there must be some form of punishment attached to it. Punishment can be in the form of a fine, incarceration, or death, or a combination of punishments.

Understanding the basics of criminal law allows for the asking of the question: Why do we have laws? A brief historical presentation is necessary to answer this.

History

The earliest penal code was the *Code of Hammurabi* (of Babylon). This code (a) provided a highly detailed legal code with instructions on appropriate procedures for the application of the codes, and (b) reflected an explicit effort to merge notions of using laws as an instrument of social change with the retributive view that those who violate the law should be punished in proportion to the degree of harm they have done.

U.S. criminal law is primarily based upon English common law, which emerged around the 12th century. English common law developed from judges ruling that certain actions or behaviors (crime) were subject to state control and sanctions. These decisions gave rise to the principle of *stare decisis,* or "let the decision stand," which we recognize today as *precedents.* Although all states' criminal laws are linked to common law, all criminal law has become recognized as statutory law.

While criminal justice is concerned with criminal law, it is important to recognize that there are two major divisions of law in the United States: criminal and civil. Emphasis of the differences and similarities between the two is prudent. The following is considered with respect to differences:

Criminal Law

The four aspects of criminal law are:

1. The major objective is to protect the public from harm resulting from criminal acts.
2. The state initiates the legal proceeding and imposes the punishment.
3. The emphasis is on the intent of the individual committing the act.
4. Guilt must be proven beyond a reasonable doubt.

Civil Law

The four major aspects of civil law are:

1. The major concern is that the injured party is compensated for any harm or injury.
2. The aggrieved party must initiate the proceeding.
3. Primary attention is given to affixing blame for producing damage.
4. Guilt is based upon the preponderance of the evidence.

Similarities

Both legal divisions seek to control people's behavior, both impose sanctions, and many acts are found to be both criminal and civil violations.

Having this knowledge allows us to return to the question, Why do we have criminal law? Perhaps it is easier to answer this question by asking it in a slightly different manner: What are the purposes of criminal law?

The responses can include:

- Reflecting change in public opinion
- Deterring crime and protecting society
- Supporting social stability and protecting the free enterprise system
- Controlling society's need to seek retribution

Furthermore, to better understand the purpose of criminal law requires recognizing the sources from which it may come. These include: common law, legislation (statutes), and administrative agencies. A requisite of all laws is that they must conform to the dictates of the U.S. and state constitutions. With this information it is now possible to examine how crimes are classified.

CLASSIFICATIONS

There are several means by which crimes are classified. The broadest classifications are *mala in se* (crimes that are inherently wrong—for example, murder) and *mala prohibitum* (offenses established by statute). However, we do not go around saying that a person committed or is guilty of a *mala in se*; we use the more common classifications, *felonies* (any offense punishable by more than one year of incarceration or death) and *misdemeanors* (up to one year incarceration/fine). What classification an act receives is determined by statute as well as the punishment. Yet how does one actually know when a crime has occurred? By recognizing what is referred to as the elements of the crime.

ELEMENTS

Defining and categorizing crime is just the beginning of what one should learn about crime. How a crime is recognized rests on the presence of its statutorily defined elements. Thus, one needs to be introduced to the concept of *corpus delicti* (body of the crime) and its key characteristics:

- The *actus reus,* or the guilty act (the physical elements associated with the performance of the offense);
- The *mens rea,* or the guilty mind (mental state when crime was committed or a failure to act occurs). The most important element of *mens rea* is **intent**. Intent can be *general, specific,* or *transferred;*
- A relationship between the *actus reus* and the *mens rea.*

In addition, one should be familiar with the concept of strict liability crimes. These are the exception to the intent rule. For a strict liability crime, intent is of no concern; the act itself is enough. Examples of this type of crime include certain traffic violations, public intoxication, or possession of illegal narcotics.

Finally, because intent, a key characteristic of a crime, translates into responsibility, it is necessary to recognize that there are certain conditions under which an individual is not held criminally responsible. This is often referred to as defenses to intent. Although there are a number of possible defenses, here are seven of the more commonly acceptable ones (albeit briefly):

1. **Insanity**—whether a person was suffering from some form of mental disease or problem that in effect made it difficult or impossible to determine whether the act committed was right or wrong (for example, someone suffering from paranoid delusions kills his roommate).

2. **Age (infancy)**—the person was not of a legally recognizable age to be able to form intent, which in many states is under the age of 10 years.
3. **Involuntary intoxication**—a person is given a drug or alcohol without his or her knowledge and then commits a criminal act because of the effects of the drug or alcohol.
4. **Duress**—a person commits a crime because he or she is being forced to do so through threat of harm to self or member(s) of the person's family (for example, a non-gang member is told he must rob a convenience store or be beaten by the gang).
5. **Necessity**—under normal conditions a person would not commit a criminal act, but it becomes a necessity for survival (for example, escape from a jail during a riot to avoid being injured or killed).
6. **Self-defense**—protecting oneself from pending harm from another (for example, when attacked by a person with a knife, you break the assailant's arm holding the knife).
7. **Entrapment**—a person commits a crime due to law enforcement coercion or actions (for example, a police officer working undercover offers to have sex with you for money; you agree and are then arrested).

Completing the discussion on criminal responsibility concludes the introductory section. From here one should have a basic understanding of the fundamentals of criminal justice and the CJS and should now be ready to advance into the individual components, starting with the most observable component in the CJS, the police.

THE POLICE COMPONENT

The focus of information about the CJS can now begin to narrow to each of the three components. Since the most recognized and observable component is the police, we will begin here. The police component can be examined through three main areas: role and organization, issues, and police and the law.

Role and Organization

To begin to understand the police subsystem, a brief historical discussion is in order. This begins by stating that today's police agencies are deeply influenced by past practices, traditions, attitudes, and so on, and were primarily influenced by our English heritage.

One of the first systems was the "hue and cry," or the watch system. Eventually it gave way to the first modern police agency, the London Metropolitan Police Department (LMPD), which became the model for future British and American police agencies.

The historical role development in America consists of colonial American police institutions (sheriff, constable, watch), none of which were considered very effective or efficient. These early institutions were ill equipped, ill trained, and corrupt. Of the three, only the watch actually provided any type of proactive police protection. The sheriff and constable were reactive. None were able to provide order maintenance, control the problem of corruption, or gain citizen respect.

Policing in America begins to change in the early part of the 19th century, in particular from 1838 to 1854. During this change and growth of modern police agencies in the U.S., politics had tremendous influence on every aspect of policing including personnel standards, recruitment, priorities, and corruption. Although early selection standards were nonexistent, jobs were obtained primarily through political contacts (patronage); there was no training, departments were ethnically dominated, and job security was limited. Yet becoming a police officer had broad appeal because it was one of the best paying jobs available.

An important consideration of this period and the changes taking place was the influence that politics had on policing, especially with respect to corruption. A reform movement began—some reforms included the creation of administrative boards and state control of some agencies. Other considerations for presentation with respect to the reform movement include:

- the Wickersham Commission which exposed the corruption and abuses of power, calling for professionalization through education, training, and technological improvements;
- August Vollmer, chief of police Berkeley, California (1905–1932), who organized the first college-level police science courses and was the first chief to hire college students;
- Richard Sylvester, president of IACP (1901–1915);
- O. W. Wilson, police chief and first author of a police administration and organization textbook;
- the FBI's adoption of a college degree being a requisite for hiring;
- Chief Richard Parker, Los Angeles P.D., and his attempt to make LAPD the model municipal police agency;
- the entry of women into policing.

Furthermore, despite all the above, it is noted that due to growing problems in police-community relations and the civil rights movement, policing became distracted from its efforts toward professionalism. The time frame this period covers is early 1900s through the 1950s, which brings us to a favorite period of police role development and change, the 1960s.

Although it is the choice of the individual, it is common to address the 1960s as the crisis period of modern policing. Activities and changes during this time included:

- New expectations about police performance accentuated by political protests,
- Racial discrimination,

- The Vietnam war,
- Sharp rises in the rate of crime,
- Landmark decisions of the U.S. Supreme Court, sometimes referred to as the due process revolution.

A summation of this period allows that society required more in the way of order maintenance and social services, as well as increased crime fighting, than at anytime previous to this, and it made for a very difficult role for police officers to fill.

The historical information can be concluded with a look at policing in the 1970s, 1980s, and today. Issues might include: continuing problems, even though officers are better trained, educated, and equipped; and the impact of unions, technological advances, and affirmative action. Despite the brief history, one should be ready for other aspects about role and organization.

Agencies

While the historical material is important, to truly better understand policing requires acknowledgment and examination of the agencies that compose the police subsystem. There are the three primary levels among which agencies are divided:

1. **Local level,** which comprises a majority of authorized police agencies and personnel in the United States, divided among municipal, metropolitan, and county agencies. The functions of each differ only by the needs of environment being served but generally include four types of service: law enforcement, crime prevention, order maintenance, and social services.
2. **State,** which was legislatively developed to deal with growing problem of crime in nonurban or unincorporated areas and consists of two basic types: full-service (State Police/Department of Public Safety) and highway patrol;

3. **Federal,** whose agencies generally are concerned with the violation of federal laws and whose role and mission is established by statute. Major federal agencies are: FBI, DEA, INS, U.S. Marshals, Customs, ATF, Secret Service, IRS, and Postal Service.

Even though there are agencies in three levels of policing, the most commonly recognized are those at the local level, in particular the municipal or city police. Therefore, the remaining discussion is primarily related to this specific type of agency and level of policing.

Organization

Municipal agencies are independent entities, each with its own structure and organizational flow. Most common is the quasi-military-like structure that offers a hierarchy and a chain of command system where ranks and responsibilities are specifically drawn. It is also usual for these agencies to be divided by tasks or functions.

Functions

Although local agencies may differ in many respects, one can still find each to be similar in its overall functions. There are four major functions:

1. **Patrol,** which is viewed as the backbone of police departments. This is the most visible manifestation of the police in the eyes of the public—with few exceptions, everyone starts out as a patrol officer. The basic functions of patrol are relatively unchanged since 1829 and include deterrence of crime, maintaining public security, and 24-hour availability for service;
2. **Investigations,** which is primarily relegated to the detective divisions—plain-clothes investigators who follow up reports turned in by patrol officers. Being a detective is a general goal of many police officers. Why?

Money, freedom, more interesting tasks, an air of elitism, and support of the crimefighter image. In reality it can be very tedious, boring, and unrewarding. Larger departments are often subdivided into subunits, such as violent and property crimes, or individual units, such as homicide, burglary, robbery, vice, et cetera. A big problem is the lack of communication between detectives and patrol officers;

3. **Traffic,** whose primary function is enforcement of the traffic code, accident investigations, and so on; and
4. **Support,** which includes divisions such as personnel, IAD, records, crime lab, communications, training, planning and research, and the like.

Obviously, the police function is more than just riding around in a marked vehicle responding to calls for assistance. To ensure that the functions are carried out correctly requires strong administration and management.

Administration and Management

Regardless of what size police agency or at what level, there are always similar problems to be found in the areas of administration and management. Problems facing police managers today are recruitment and selection (debate over requirements such as education, physical, et cetera), affirmative action, salary competition, developing effective police managers, and improving police productivity/effectiveness.

Overall, the role and organization of the police component is much more complex than one might initially perceive. As it has been demonstrated, there are various levels of policing, and each must deal with organization, functions, and administration and management. Still, one could argue that it is the myriad issues in policing that garner more attention—and rightfully so. This may be especially true when one considers the possible linkage to criminology of many of these issues.

Issues

In this section, an exploration is offered of a variety of issues for which debate among, by, and between academics, practitioners, and nonpolice individuals is relatively common. Because of the number of issues and the fact that what is important to one may not be to another, only limited specifics about each are provided here. However, it is enough to sustain a basic understanding of the police and contemplate the possible link (offered in the form of a question) to criminology.

They include, but are not limited to:

1. **Brutality**—where an officer uses excess force or language against another while performing his or her duties. (LINK: Is brutality used more against specific races or ethnicities?)
2. **Corruption**—misuse of the powers of the position for personal gain, such as accepting a bribe to not write a ticket. (LINK: Why is corruption so pervasive in policing?)
3. **Use of deadly force**—(LINK: Is it used more against one group than another?)
4. **Discrimination**—(LINK: Who is discriminated against more and what are the impacts toward crime?)
5. **Police personality**—policing may attract certain types of individuals. (LINK: Why are some people attracted to policing and others not, and how does that effect how they deal with crime?)
6. **Police subculture**—as with many subcultures, there are specific norms and values that are shared. (LINK: What effect do these norms and values have on enforcing the law?)
7. **Police officer styles**—how an officer goes about doing his or her job. (LINK: Do differing styles correlate with types of arrests?)
8. **Discretion**—(LINK: How does it influence arrests?)

9. **Educational requirements for recruits**—(LINK: Does education effect how one views crime and therefore, how he or she enforces the law?)
10. **Women and minorities**—(LINK: How are they treated?)
11. **Job stress**—(LINK: What effect does this have on enforcing the law?);
12. **Police-community relations**—(LINK: Are police-community relations directly linked to crime enforcement?)
13. **Violence**—by police officers and against police officers. (LINK: Are police officers who work in high crime areas more prone to violence against suspects?)

It should be apparent that the topics introduced are just one person's choices. Nevertheless they are believed to be mainstays in the study of policing and have some possible interesting links to criminology. Yet in spite of this fact, these issues are not as demanding as is the relationship between the police and the law, which unlike the issues is not as subjective to interpretation or individual preference. Actually, it is viewed by some as one of the most relevant aspects of policing to address.

Police and the Law

The full application of the law by police officers revolves around the commission of a crime (again, a mainstay of criminology). There are four key elements to understanding how the police and law interact: detection, search and seizure, arrest, and interrogation.

Detection

Understanding this element can begin with answering this question: How do the police become aware of a crime? The three primary means are by (a) reports by complainants, (b) complaints by witnesses/concerned parties, and (c) personal observation or investigation by the officer. Once a crime has been reported, an investigation must be conducted in order to ascertain all the facts/ evidence. The obtaining of the evidence is a critical part of an investigation. Without sufficient evidence, a crime cannot be shown to have been committed. There are several ways an officer can obtain evidence: interviewing, interrogation, surveillance, and physical collection. Once evidence is obtained, the investigation should lead to an arrest, but first the evidence must be gathered.

Search and Seizure

To successfully complete an investigation, there is often the need to collect evidence. Evidence collection is governed by the search and seizure requirements of the Fourth Amendment of the Constitution, whose basic underlying premise protects us from illegally obtained evidence being used against us in a court of law.

Additional topics of concern are probable cause, search warrants, plain view, consent, search incident to an arrest, and other warrantless searches (stop and frisk, automobile, and electronic surveillance). A full discussion of each is neither required nor prudent at this juncture, within the text. However, they are topics one needs to be knowledgeable of and should be discussed at some length in the classroom setting. These topics make understanding the next topic—arrest—much easier.

Arrest

An interesting element of the law is the concept of an arrest, which occurs when a police officer believes to have sufficient proof that a crime has been or is about to be committed and the officer intends to restrain a suspect, or when an individual's freedom is deprived and he or she cannot voluntarily leave. The authority to arrest and by whom, how, and when an arrest can be made is generally described in each state's code of criminal procedures. Other topics of interest include the use of discretion and false arrest.

Interrogation

The most common procedure by police officers upon arresting someone is to interrogate him or her. However, prior to interrogation, the police must warn the subject of his or her constitutional right against self-incrimination. Although governed by the Fifth Amendment, it was not until the 1966 case of *Miranda v. Arizona* that the courts reinforced its necessity. Prior to *Miranda*, the obtaining of a confession was done through a variety of methods that are no longer tolerated—for example, with an arrest, evidence obtained from an illegally obtained confession is inadmissible.

As a result of *Miranda*, many observers were concerned that the court had gone too far in protecting the rights of the defendant. Yet to date there has been little empirical support for this position, and in reality it appears to have had very little negative impact. The major issue with *Miranda* today is under what circumstances should *Miranda* be given.

The section on police and law can be summarized in this manner: The law is a very important aspect of policing; not only must they enforce it, but they must remain within legal realms when enforcing it. Having reached this point, one has completed reviewing the basic lessons on the police component. This allows us to move to the next component or phase of the CJS, the courts.

THE COURTS COMPONENT

It was previously noted that while the court subsystem is often the least funded of the three CJS components, it generally has the most responsibilities surrounding crime and criminal behavior. To adequately understand this component, it is best to examine it among four main parts: structures, pretrial processes, adversaries, and the criminal trial.

Remaining consistent, a definition of the concept is required. However, defining the courts is not as simplistic as other concepts because one can easily debate as to whether the definition is mythical (theoretical) or realistic (practical). This is one possible definition to begin study from:

> The criminal court is an arena of decision making in the criminal justice system—it is here that bail, trials, plea bargaining, and sentencing all occur. It provides a process designed to provide an open and impartial forum for deciding justice. A specific set of rules and procedures are followed in an attempt to provide a clear, objective, and fair outcome.[5]

This definition opens a path for discussion as to how realistically it defines today's court system. Furthermore, it allows for discussion of the two main views of the court process: **traditional,** which sees the courts as a setting for adversarial procedure that is fair and formalized and is controlled by the laws of criminal procedure and rules of evidence, and **realistic,** where the court is viewed as a system that encourages the settling of matters in the simplest, quickest, and most efficient manner possible. This of course requires recognizing a current view of the court process as nothing more than "assembly-line" justice.

Structures

By completing the definitional discussion, one can now examine the actual structuring of the court systems, of which there are two:

1. **The State Court System**—each state maintains its own court system and structure—therefore we have 50 separate court systems. Each state system is basically a trilateral structure: The *lowest tier* (courts of limited jurisdiction—minor misdemeanors, city ordinances, traffic, and small claims) is usually not a court of record

---

[5.] Again, this is a definition I've adopted from another source that I can no longer identify. However, it is not my own.

and penalties are often restricted to fines. The *second tier* (courts of general jurisdiction—the basic trial court—often referred to as district, circuit, superior) usually handles felonies but can hear all types of cases. They often are specialized—criminal, civil, family, juvenile, and so on. The *final tier* (appellate courts) can be viewed as two divisions—intermediate and supreme. These courts hear appeals to determine whether an error in procedure was made, and if an error is found, the court can order a new trial, allow the defendant to go free, or uphold the original verdict. The state's supreme court is the ultimate court of appeal within each state—controversial decisions can be taken into the federal system; and

2. **The Federal Court System,** which also consists of three levels. The *lowest level* are the district courts, of which there are 94. Each state has at least one district court (plus Puerto Rico, D.C., Guam, Virgin Islands, and the N. Mariana Islands). These are trial courts with **original jurisdiction** over all cases involving alleged violations of federal statutes. There are nearly 600 district judges who are appointed by the president and confirmed by the Senate and who serve for life. In addition there are over 400 U.S. magistrates who have the power to conduct arraignments and may set bail, issue warrants, and try petty offenders and some misdemeanants. The *second level* is the U.S. Court of Appeals, of which there are 12 (also called circuit courts because the federal system is divided into eleven circuits plus D.C.). One hundred fifty judges staff the various courts. The *final level* is the U.S. Supreme Court. Created under Article III of the Constitution (Judiciary Act of 1789 provided for one chief justice and 5 associates), the U. S. Supreme Court was set by Congress in 1869 at nine members, where it has remained.

Discussion of the federal system is not complete without a more in-depth view of the U.S. Supreme Court. It is often best to begin by identifying the more famous U.S. Supreme Courts, such as the **Marshall Court** (1801–1835) (Decided *Marbury v. Madison*); the **Hughes Court** (1930–1941), which had to withstand Roosevelt's court packing scheme; the **Warren Court** (1953–1969), which oversaw the beginning of civil rights and due process landmark cases); the **Burger Court** (1969–1979), which continued the due process revolution); and the current **Rehnquist Court** (1979–), which is more conservative than its predecessor. Further discussion would also address the Court's jurisdictions, ways to obtain review, and making decisions.

In short, the court system is based on two systems, local and federal, each of which operate through a three-tier system consisting of trial, intermediate appeals, and final appellate courts. The overseer of both systems is the U.S. Supreme Court.

After learning about the structures of the courts, one can now be introduced to the main courtroom character: the judge. The judge is the senior officer in the court whose duties are varied and extensive and who has control and influence over the other CJ agencies and personnel. Furthermore, the judge is often considered the symbol of justice for most Americans. Duties include presiding over trials and all the tasks involved therein, administration of the court and its docket, and supervison over probation and indirectly over police and prosecution. A judge is supposed to be a highly qualified individual—which is not always the case. A judge is often a political animal who is either elected or appointed, and although all judges are supposed to be lawyers who have passed the bar exam, many magistrates do not fit this criteria (state level only). Because of their extensive responsibilities, courtroom administrators have been hired to assist the judge in the daily operations of the court. Additional topics which may be open to discussion in this area often include the requirements for becoming a judge and selection to the bench both at the state and federal levels. With the basics completed, the pretrial process can now be introduced.

Pretrial Process

Having laid the foundation as to how the courts are structured, the next step is usually to review the processes that occur prior to a trial taking place, which in reality is a rarity. It is during the pretrial process that a majority of cases are disposed of, usually through two basic means: (a) dismissal and (b) plea bargaining. It is best to begin the process from point of arrest. Several procedures are identifiable. They often start with the booking of the suspect (when the arrested person is taken to jail and processed in); preliminary hearings (where a judge hears whether there is enough probable cause to file charges); grand jury (a body used in some jurisdictions to determine whether there is enough evidence for an indictment); arraignment (where the arrestee is officially advised of the charges against him or her); bail (method of being kept out of jail until the trial is over), and plea bargaining (seen as the bread and butter of the court system, it allows a suspect to make a deal that may render an easier punishment than if convicted in court). From here, we can now address the two other main characters in the court system: the prosecutor and the defense attorney—more commonly known as the adversaries.

The Adversaries

From the pretrial processes, one can now look at the two additional main actors in the courtroom, the prosecutor and the defense attorney, aptly referred to as the adversaries. Beginning with the prosecutor, it should be noted that he or she is a highly visible, generally strong, political individual, considered the top law enforcement official of his/her jurisdictional area—either elected or appointed. (The U.S. attorney and the state's attorney are generally appointed; the county and district attorney are generally elected.) Additional review of the prosecutor can include the roles, duties, types of prosecutors, and discretionary power. This position can be briefly summarized in this manner: The prosecutor plays several roles with a variety of activities, with reasons for decisions not always obvious but usually dependent upon the evidence.

The adversarial counterpart of the prosecutor is the defense attorney, whose existence is due to the constitutional rights of the accused to have the right to counsel (Sixth Amendment). Several court cases that have clarified this right even further should be recognized, such as *Powell v. Alabama* (1932): right in capital cases—counsel appointed for indigent; *Gideon v. Wainwright* (1963): felonious actors—if unable to afford counsel, one is appointed); *Escobedo v. Illinois* (1964): when questioning goes from informational to accusatory, one has a right to counsel; *Argersinger v. Hamlin* (1972): regardless of the offense committed, right to counsel exists; and any other more recent case that the instructor finds appropriately applicable. Additional inquiry of the defense attorney includes the long-standing image, types of defense lawyers, duties, and the criminal bar. Having established the structures, pretrial processes, and the actors, we can now look at the last part of the courts system, the trial.

Criminal Trial

Prior to actually looking at the steps of the trial, one should become familiar with an individuals right's as they apply to a trial. These rights include *the right to a jury trial* as granted by the Sixth Amendment; *the right to counsel*; *the right to self-representation* (although the courts traditionally encourage defendants to accept counsel, an individual could, technically, represent himself); and *the right to a speedy trial*.

Basic Steps

The trial process is a structured adversary proceeding in which the prosecutor will use testimony, evidence, statements, confessions, and so on to prove guilt beyond a reasonable doubt. The defense will attempt to refute the state and protect the defen-

dant's rights while the judge promotes an orderly, impartial proceeding. There are nine basic steps to trial:

1. Jury selection
2. Opening statements
3. Presentation of the state's case
4. Presentation of the defense
5. Closing arguments
6. Instruction to the jury
7. The verdict
8. Sentencing
9. Appeals

This portion can usually be concluded with a discussion
about sentencing (punishment), including looking at the traditional reasons why we sentence or punish (retribution, isolation,
deterrence, restitution, and rehabilitation). This discussion also
addresses the types of punishment we employ in the U.S. (imprisonment, fines, probation, death penalty, others such as restitution,
house arrest or electronic monitoring, treatment programs, and
community service).

This concludes the part on criminal trials and completes the
material advocated under the courts component. The last section of this chapter examines two topics that are often the last
ones presented in a criminal justice course and in the textbooks:
corrections and juveniles. Despite their positioning, they are
probably the strongest linked criminal justice components to
criminology.

THE CORRECTIONS
AND JUVENILES COMPONENTS

From a teaching perspective, by the time most instructors reach
these components, assuming they are presenting them in the
order laid forth here, there is usually very little time left to teach

them. However, even addressed briefly, as is this text, all the following topics deserve some attention: probation, corrections, parole, and juvenile justice.

Probation[6]

The first step is to define probation as the practice of maintaining convicted criminal offenders in the community under supervision of court authority. This can then be followed by a brief historical review; analyses of the concept, which refers to a sentence, a status or process, and an organization; the philosophy of probation (allows offenders to prove themselves, receive a second chance, and establish proper forms of behavior); the provisions of probation; probation officers; the currently expanding role of probation to include restitution, volunteers, and intensive supervision; and revocation.

Corrections

It is probably best to begin by discussing early correctional approaches, primarily early punishments, such as flogging, mutilation, branding, public humiliation, workhouses, and transportation. This can be followed by the introduction to jails, which includes history (Walnut Street Jail), crowding, and other general problems.

Jails are then proceeded by prisons, which is more of a correctional entity than jails. Therefore, content usually can include

---

[6.] Strictly from a teaching perspective, I find it best to begin this section by noting that although probation is actually a tool of the courts, it is common for most introductory texts to locate probation within the correctional arena, sometimes followed immediately by the section on parole. Therefore, I, too, will usually incorporate probation into the corrections section but will add my caveats of why it can be taught either as part of the courts or part of corrections.

the emergence of prisons using a breakdown by eras borrowed from Schmalleger (1997) (See Table 4–2), the levels of security, privatization, federal prisons, and community corrections. Other components suggested for consumption are prison life, which often includes the subcultures, socialization/prisonization, prison code, argot, and prison society; prison staff, who are usually not well-trained and are mainly concerned with custody and control and whose culture is often influenced by potential threats from the prisoner culture; riots (whose causes have been linked to insensitivity on the part of administrators, neglect, violence brought in from the streets—in particular, gang and racial violence—dehumanized conditions, and power struggles); the stages of the riot are explosion, organization (into inmate-led groups), confrontation (with authority), termination, and reaction and explanation; women in prison whose issues include overcrowding, drugs, social structure (artificial families), and violence; prisoners' rights and intervention of the courts; and other issues, such as AIDS (and homosexuality), age, disabilities; and how to restructure prisons so that there is either more punishment or a better rehabilitation effort.

Table 4–2.   Prison History by Eras

1790–1825	Penitentiary era (solitary confinement, penitence; Pennsylvania system);
1825–1876	Mass prison (congregate fashion; Auburn system);
1876–1890	Reformatory (use of intermediate sentencing and belief in rehabilitation);
1890–1935	Industrial prison (production of marketable goods);
1935–1945	Punitive (security and belief that inmates owe debt to society);
1945–1967	Treatment;
1967–1980	Community-based
1980–1990	Warehousing (no hope of rehabilitation); and
1990–****	Overcrowding (early release, punishment).

Parole

Viewed as the partner to probation, yet an explicit tool of the corrections subsystem, parole is the planned community release and supervision of incarcerated criminals prior to the actual expiration of their sentences. Here topics generally include history, the extent of the use of parole, supervision (parole board and parole officers), conditions of parole, the effectiveness of parole, and parole revocation.

Juvenile Justice (Delinquency)

The last portion of the corrections component as well as for the whole course is an examination of juvenile justice and delinquency. It might begin with a brief historical perspective (the early years featured no preferential treatment for children; in early America, Puritan influence and harsh punishment; Enlightenment era in the late 18th century led to increased social concern for a child's well-being; institutional era). This is followed by looking at problems, such as drugs, gangs, runaways, sexual abuse, other abuses, and suicide; the juvenile courts (initiated in Massachusetts in 1870; the Illinois Juvenile Court Act of 1899 became the model for juvenile statutes throughout the nation); how children are categorized (delinquent—law violators, dependent—abandoned, neglected, abused, and status offenders—violators of crimes that apply only to juveniles—for example, truancy, curfew, minor possession of alcohol); legislation and court cases (*Kent v. U.S.*—minimal due process, *In re Gault*—extension of due process, *In re Winship*—guilt beyond a reasonable doubt, *McKeiver v. Pennsylvania*—denial of jury entitlements, *Breed v. Jones*—restricted transfers from juvenile status to adult status, and *Schall v. Martin*—preventive detention); and today's problems, such as gangs, violence, younger offenders, revolving door, and lax punishments.

In general, there are many important aspects to corrections and juveniles, so much so that neither this chapter, or, in many cases, time in the classroom, can do them justice. Still, enough has been shared so that a person should now have a much better idea of what is involved and can be begin to establish his or her own thoughts as to how the two components might link with criminology.

CONCLUSION

As with criminology, the basic contents of a criminal justice course offers a plethora of topics. How those topics are offered in writing or taught depends heavily on authors and instructors. Yet regardless of how the material is communicated, for it to be useful to an individual, especially one pursuing a degree in criminal justice or criminology, the material should most definitely address, at minimum, the topics, concepts, and issues shared in this chapter. Otherwise, criminal justice students are at a disadvantage when they enroll in advanced courses designed to focus specifically on a particular component or issue.

Furthermore, they will have a difficult time understanding the linkage or relationship with and to criminology. However, this is a task the remaining chapters should assist in accomplishing.

FOR THE CRITICAL THINKER

1. Having completed the introduction to the content of criminal justice, how would you define it as an academic discipline?
2. What areas of criminal justice appear to be the most important? Least important? Why?
3. How does the study of criminal justice from an academic perspective improve one's understanding of it as a social focus? What, if anything, is missing that could further improve one's understanding?
4. Why is it that the police component receives more societal criticism than any other component? Why do the

courts appear to have a greater role in the CJS but receive less money? What is, realistically, the role of corrections?

5. If you had to explain or describe criminal justice in the United States to someone from another country, how would you do it? What would you emphasize? Ignore? Explain why.

5

Comparing, Contrasting, and Intertwining

The first four chapters of this book have established two concepts, criminology and criminal justice, as ideals of social focus and as academic disciplines. They have examined the evolution, definition, and contextual nature of both. In other words, the foundation has been set to accomplish the objectives of the last three chapters—that is, to compare, contrast, intertwine, apply, and speculate for the future.

This chapter looks at both disciplines from comparative, contrasting, and intertwining perspectives. Furthermore, the discussion will focus on how, in many respects, there is much more similarity between the two areas and the importance of recognizing this.

AS SOCIAL FOCI

Starting with both concepts as social foci, recall that as a social focus, criminology is the exploration of the evolution of criminal behavior that requires the existence of criminal justice as a social construct. Criminal justice as a social focus is the creation, application, and enforcement of criminal law in an effort to maintain social order. As social foci, both are several hundred years in the making, with their roots planted and evolving from early European history. This history demonstrates how criminology and criminal justice are responses to society's need to control and understand certain types of behavior, in particular what society recognizes as criminal behavior. Evolving as social foci, criminology and criminal justice have become rooted in society's attempt to maintain social order.

Consider that the underlying foundation of criminology and criminal justice is the law. Any changes occurring in the law often require changes in criminology and criminal justice. For example, when a new criminal law is enacted, such as driving under the influence of alcohol or drugs, from a criminological perspective, focus can center on why an individual would drive in an impaired condition, and why do it more than the first time a person is apprehended. The criminal justice focus would be on how to prevent, deter, apprehend, prosecute, and punish those who have violated the law. In either case, new laws create new implications for both sides.

What happens when punishment for an already existing criminal law is increased? Criminologists need to examine the ramifications and influences of this change on criminal behavior, both socially and on individuals. The justician has to consider what effects this change would or does have on specifically related CJS components, such as the police (enforcement issues), the courts (sentencing issues), and the jails and prisons (space), not to mention the effect on the adversarial counterparts.

The law is the key catalyst to what occurs in criminology and criminal justice, giving both their existence as social foci.

Any changes in the law affect both. Comparatively, neither can exist without the law and the resulting criminal behavior.

In contrast, of the two, criminal justice has evolved and existed much longer as a social focus than criminology. The history of criminal justice dates back to earliest biblical times, and criminology really does not receive much attention until the mid-18th century. In addition, as social foci, criminal justice garners more attention from the common citizen because of the influence and impact it can have on the individual's life. Criminology, or why people commit crime, is of more interest to academics than to John Q. Citizen. However, because understanding criminal behavior can help improve criminal justice, it allows criminology to remain as a social focus.

There are probably many more similarities and differences identifiable between criminology and criminal justice as social foci. However, it is the major aspects, the law and its attendant behaviors, without which comparisons and contrasts are moot. The importance of both as social foci is evident and leads to a greater interest of both as academic disciplines.

AS ACADEMIC DISCIPLINES

To start, reviewing the working definitions is prudent. *Criminology* is the scientific approach to the study of crime as a social phenomenon—that is, the theoretical application involving the study of the nature and extent of criminal behavior—and *criminal justice* is the applied and scientific study of the practical applications of criminal behavior—that is, the actions, policies, or functions of the agencies within the criminal justice system charged with addressing this behavior. Chapters 3 and 4 presented the general content of both disciplines, finding that there are broad and extensive differences. So, as academic disciplines, how do they compare?

Comparing

First, both disciplines support a scientific approach to study. Hypotheses, theories and explanations as to the functioning, behaviors, and existence of each discipline's main elements are abundant. The gathering and analyzing of data in an attempt to support or disprove these hypotheses, theories, and explanations is similar in both disciplines. There are four main methods employed: survey research, observational studies, life histories or case studies, and record studies. All have long been considered mainstays of scientific methodology, thus reinforcing the scientific nature of both disciplines. While criminology and criminal justice compare in their support of the use of the scientific approach to the study of crime and criminal behavior, which will be further demonstrated in the next chapter, a point of contrast is that they might use them toward different means.

Contrasting

Where criminology and criminal justice contrast the most is for what the scientific approach is used to discover, prove, or support. That is, criminology wants to know more about why someone is criminal, whereas criminal justice wants to known more about what to do with the criminal and how the different parts of the CJS are functioning. Again, this will be reinforced in the next chapter.

A second academic aspect is that both disciplines are concerned with criminality. Both sides agree that criminality is wrong and that society has a right to address those who commit a crime. How they go about its study is what separates the two.

Criminology is more interested in offering reasons as to why crime exists and why individuals become criminal. Criminologists believe that they can provide answers that can be translated into a means to control and treat criminal behavior. Justicians, on the other hand, are more interested in simply controlling behavior through enforcement and punishment and why, often, the methods seem to have little effect. They are also more interested in the individuals and institutions that serve to address the criminal than the crime or the criminal behavior itself. This difference of interests is what distinguishes and establishes the biggest contrast of the two disciplines into theoretical and practical applications.

As pointed out in Chapter 3, criminology as an academic discipline is concerned with providing reasons for why individuals commit crime. This effort is supported through the offering of explanations (often in the way of theories) for the behavior. It was suggested that there are a multitude of possible reasons for why individuals commit crime. As an academic discipline, the major interest is to understand the "why" and "what for."

Criminal justice is concerned with the "how to"—that is, how to stop, enforce, and punish those who are identified as having committed criminal behavior. Academically, it focuses on those institutions and agencies charged with meeting or fulfilling the "how to." Therefore, a major point of contrast between the two disciplines is the focus of inquiry—criminology deals with the behavior that often leads to an arrest, conviction, and punishment; criminal justice is interested in how to deal with the behavior by means of arrest, conviction, and incarceration and how the supporting units are handling it.

Other similarities as academic disciplines include the fact that both disciplines enjoy a healthy following of academics and students. Yet in some cases these disciplines are still struggling for full acceptance from other social sciences. Nevertheless, both provide scholarly research that addresses main concerns in criminal justice and criminology and offer assistance to CJS practitioners through research and consulting. Furthermore, it is relatively common for students in both disciplines to continue to graduate studies and/or to accept employment in some component of the criminal justice system. However, this aspect can be an area of contention for academics, particularly criminologists, because it appears that more students believe a criminal justice degree will be more marketable than a criminology degree.[1] Reality begs to

---

[1] Probably one of the reasons that students believe this is because it is common to see advertisements for positions in the CJS where if a bachelor's degree is a requirement, a criminal justice major is often preferred. This stipulation demonstrates lack of understanding as to the similarities of the two majors by those practitioners doing the hiring.

differ in that both degrees are valuable and have similar effects toward improving employment chances. Still, it should be noted that another difference is that criminology students are often more interested in research-oriented work than the criminal justice students, who want to become police, probation, parole, or correctional officers, for which there is a greater demand than research-oriented positions. However, this is just one contrasting point. Where criminology and criminal justice most often tend to contrast, at least on the surface as academic disciplines, is best recognized in the establishment of university or college programs and the course requirements associated with a college degree in the respective discipline.

Since the 1970s when both disciplines began taking serious strides toward becoming singularly, recognizable programs or departments of criminology or criminal justice, the battle as to which it should be continues. Criminology has had to shake the shadow of sociology while criminal justice has made the transition from a police or training-oriented approach to the more global criminal justice. Previously it was suggested that there are more university or college criminal justice programs than criminology programs. This can be affirmed through the examination of program titles listed in a variety of college directories. Criminal justice programs do outnumber criminology programs. However, perhaps this distinction of program title may be misleading. Observing the missions and goals of these programs may actually prove that titles are deceiving and that the name difference is simply a question of semantics. To reinforce this point, an examination of a few programs' mission and/or goals should help shed some light on this possibility.[2]

Beginning with the oldest recognized "criminal justice" program's literature, the State University of New York at Albany (SUNYA) School of Criminal Justice, indicates:

[2.]   The five programs being used should not be viewed as representative. They were simply chosen at random (not even scientifically) to help demonstrate the point.

The School is committed to the interdisciplinary study of criminal justice. The major emphasis is sophisticated research on crime measurement and causation, as well as research into questions of appropriate and effective methods of crime control in a democratic society. All types of crime and juvenile delinquency are the focus of study, and a total systems approach is utilized to analyze, assess, and suggest changes in our crime control system. The School of Criminal Justice aims to:

- Offer rigorous and comprehensive doctoral and masters education at the highest possible level,
- Offer undergraduate education sufficiently broad to fulfill the requirements of a liberal arts education and to prepare students for graduate and law schools,
- Conduct scholarship and research to enhance the understanding of social problems and their potential solutions, and
- Provide public service rooted in research. ([http://www.scj.albany.edu:90/school.htm], 01/1997, p. 2)

The SUNYA program, although called criminal justice, appears to be strongly oriented toward theory and research. This is a direction one would expect from a criminology program. In comparison, the criminal justice program at California State University at Long Beach (CSULB) advises:

The program in criminal justice offers the bachelor of science degree to individuals interested in seeking a comprehensive education leading to a professional career in criminal justice. The program is designed to accommodate the needs of the continuing student, the transfer student, and the experienced criminal justice practitioner. (CSULB website: [edu:70/00/catalog/current/dept/crim/crim-req], 10/1996, p. 1)

Notice that the main thrust of the CSULB program is toward educating those interested in or currently employed in the CJS—an obviously different approach than the criminal justice program at SUNYA. How do both of these compare to programs touted as "criminology"?

The criminology program at the University of South Florida (USF) advocates:

> The major in criminology provides students with an in-depth exposure to the total criminal justice system including law enforcement, detention, the judiciary, corrections, and probation and parole. The program concentrates on achieving balance in the above aspects of the system from the perspective of the criminal justice professional, the offender, and society. The program provides a solid background in the theory, issues, and methodology comprising criminology. ([http://www.rmit.usf.edu/usfugs/cat9596/crim.htm], 01/1997, p. 1)

Like the SUNYA program, there appears to be a strong theoretical approach to USF's program. Yet it is also interested in preparing a student for possible employment in the CJS: "The objective of the undergraduate program in criminology is to develop a sound educational basis either for graduate work or for professional training in one or more of the specialized areas comprising the modern urban Criminal Justice System" (p. 1). Despite the reference to practical preparation, as expected from a criminology program it does appear to make preparation for graduate school its first priority. Can the same be said for other criminology programs?

Although labeled as a criminology program, observe the objectives of the Department of Criminology at Indiana University of Pennsylvania (IUP).

> The program in Criminology has a fivefold objective:
>
> 1. The education of students for employment and leadership in the expanding field of criminology and criminal justice.
> 2. The education of presently employed criminal justice personnel who recognize a need for furthering their education.

3. The instruction of students who wish to acquire an understanding of the processes of criminal justice as a cultural part of their higher education.
4. The instruction of students who wish to prepare for graduate study and/or research in criminology.
5. A curriculum that provides an excellent foundation for students preparing for a career in law. ([http://www.iup.edu/schedu/catalog/humss/d-crim.htmlx], 01/97, p. 1)

As with CSULB and USF, the IUP program appears to emphasize that the education offered will assist those seeking employment or those already employed within the CJS. Yet it, too, is interested in preparing individuals for graduate work or to conduct research. However, the emphasis seems to be on employment.

Finally, what about those departments or programs whose titles tends to indicate support of both criminal justice and criminology? Is this where the future might lie? An example of this model is found at East Tennessee State University (ETSU) in the Department of Criminal Justice and Criminology. ETSU's program objectives are:

1. To develop a critical understanding of the crime problem and the role and function of the criminal justice system in a democratic society.
2. To provide courses of instruction that complement the education received by students in related disciplines.
3. To prepare students for professional service in the criminal justice system.
4. To provide an opportunity for persons currently serving in criminal justice professions to advance their level of education.

The criminal justice and criminology curriculum is highly interdisciplinary, encompassing the study of law, the social and behavioral sciences, and other academic areas. Consistent with the above objectives, the curriculum seeks a careful balance of theoretical inquiry and applied knowledge

and features a core curriculum that all majors are required
to complete. (Obtained through the ETSU website)

The objectives of the ETSU program are very similar to those
of the other programs. The emphasis on employment and graduate work are consistent. So how does this program differ from the
others? At first glance, it would appear that the only major difference is that both terms—criminal justice and criminology—are
used in the title of the program. The objectives are quite similar.
Does this mean that the other programs are mistitled? Or are they
truly different in some other way? While the mission statements
and objectives seem to support little difference, perhaps the
course requirements indicate otherwise.

It has become a common perception that most criminology programs require students to take courses that are more
theoretically oriented; that is, they deal with speculations and
hypotheticals. Examples of courses for the criminology major
might include: Introduction to Criminology, Principles of
Criminal Behavior, Juvenile Delinquency, and Penology. In
contrast, it is perceived that criminal justice students are more
likely to be required to take such courses as Introduction to
Criminal Justice,[3] and introductory courses in policing or law
enforcement, corrections, courts, and juvenile justice. Yet how
true are these perceptions? Is there a major difference in the
types of courses required between criminology and criminal
justice programs? It is suggested that in examining the required
core[4] courses of the previously identified programs that there is
some evidence that indicates the only real difference is, again, a
question of semantics.

[3.] A point of clarification: There are some who might argue that there is little difference
between introductory criminology and criminal justice courses. However, Chapters 3
and 4 demonstrate that there is a considerable difference in the content of these courses.

[4.] By core courses, I am referring to those courses designated as being required of all
students in the major.

At SUNYA, students must take a minimum of 27 credits in criminal justice or approved equivalents. Among these 27 credits, 3 must be in statistics and 3 in research methods, while 9 must be in courses designated at 400 level or above. Prior to entry into the major, students must take and pass with a "C" or above one of two designated introductory courses: Introduction to the Nature of Crime and its Control (which appears to be an introductory criminology course) or Introduction to the Criminal Justice Process (which appears to be a standard introductory criminal justice course).

CSULB students are required to take a minimum of 42 units of criminal justice course work, of which 27 are designated as core and 3 are for the prerequisite (to all courses) class: The Criminal Justice System in Society. The core courses include the following titles:

- Contemporary Issues in Criminal Justice
- Statistics in Criminal Justice Administration
- Security Systems
- Advanced Criminal Law
- Theories of Crime Causation, Prevention, and Control
- Correctional Systems
- Introduction to Research Methods in Criminal Justice
- Enforcement Systems
- Internship

At USF criminology students are required to have a minimum of 39 designated semester hours. The required or equivalent courses are:

- Survey of the Criminal Justice System*
- Substantive Criminal Law*
- Theories of Criminal Behavior*
- Patterns of Criminal Behavior*
- Juvenile Justice Systems
- American Correctional Systems

- Research Methods (choice of two courses)
- American Law Enforcement Systems
- Seminar in Criminology

(*These courses are referred to as gateway courses and must be taken before any other courses can be taken.)

The students interested in a criminology degree from IUP must have 36 hours in the major. These six courses are required for all majors:

- Survey of Criminology
- Criminal Law
- Theories of Complex Criminal Justice Organizations
- Research Methods
- Theoretical Criminology
- Contemporary Issues

Finally, ETSU criminal justice/criminology students are all required to take a total of 42 hours in the major. Eighteen of the hours (six courses) must be:

- Introduction to Criminal Justice
- Research Methods for Criminal Justice and Criminology
- Criminal Law
- Statistics for Criminal Justice and Criminology
- Criminal Justice Ethics
- Criminology

Again, although these five programs are not offered as a representative sample of all such programs, one could easily argue that if they were representative, the comparison and contrasts do prove interesting. All five require some type of introductory (either criminal justice or criminology), criminal law, and research method courses. It also appears that all require a theory course. In addition, while the number of core courses differ, their goal is similar: to provide students with a well-rounded foundation for the study of criminal justice or criminology. Furthermore, while the titles of courses differed, the contents' descriptions were quite similar, and if they were not part of the core, they were elective courses or required as part of a track (for example, law enforcement or corrections).

In essence, the information available suggests that there is actually little difference between a criminal justice and criminology program, especially with respect to required courses. Yet there continues to be debate as to offering and attaining one degree over the other. If the mission and objectives are similar, and the course requirements are similar, what then is the difference between the two disciplines as academic programs? Perhaps the overriding factor for students when it comes to deciding to pursue one or the other is the employment aspect.

If students are provided information that allows them to compare and contrast a criminal justice versus a criminology program, they really might discover little difference in content. Ultimately, the end result becomes one of employment focus: Students with criminology degrees are more often required to pursue graduate work in criminology with a goal of becoming a scholar, academician, and or researcher, while for criminal justice students, although graduate study is available, it is not yet a standard requirement for employment in the CJS, unless the person is interested in becoming a criminal justice academician. Therefore, pursuing a criminal justice degree seems to have greater appeal for those seeking jobs as practitioners rather than as researchers or academicians. This is particularly true for the undergraduate student. Graduate study takes on a slightly different context and creates other implications because the goal here is usually to become a college professor and/or to do research. This brings us to our last academic issue: the criminologist versus the justician as an academician.

By this point it should be clear that there is a distinction between those who are criminologists and those who are criminal justice practitioners. As Conrad (1979) pointed out:

> A career in criminology is interesting, better paid than it used to be, and different from the careers of a court administrator, a probation officer, a correctional commissioner, or a police chief. To qualify as a criminologist does no more than to make a scholar eligible for work as a university teacher or a specialist in research. Credentials as a criminologist have no relevance for work in any of the professional or technical disciplines of criminal justice. (p. 11)

If one were to apply Conrad's statement today, one would have to assume that only criminologists taught and practitioners where just that, practitioners: police, probation, parole, or correctional officers; CJ administrators; lawyers; and judges. It would also mean that distinctively different educational tracts would be necessary, which for many years existed. For example, the criminologist would be schooled in a variety of topics, such as sociology, psychology, anthropology, political science, and criminal law. In addition, extensive knowledge of research methodology and statistics were required. This is still true today.

On the other hand, the practitioner was more often trained than educated. Arrest, law, search and seizure, constitutional rights, self-defense, and firearms were just a few of the more commonly offered course topics. While this may have prepared the individual for working in the CJS, it did little for preparing this person to teach in an academic setting. Yet for many years the criminal justice "academic" was often an experienced practitioner with little formal education. As undergraduate degrees in criminal justice became available, these "academics" now were practitioners with bachelor's degrees but still were nowhere close to the level of scholarly preparation that criminologists received. Nevertheless, with the growth of criminal justice as an academic interest, the need for teachers with an ability to relate to the practical applications and have advanced educational levels became a necessity. This has led to the creation of many graduate programs with a criminal justice emphasis.

Today's criminal justice academicians or criminal justice specialists (Adler, 1995) have moved far away from their practitioner predecessors and much closer to their criminologist counterparts. Therefore, who are criminal justice specialists? The best response, to date, was provided by one of the better known criminologists and justicians of current time (the past 20 years), Freda Adler.

Dr. Adler proposed that criminal justice specialists are best defined by the following:

- Beneficiaries of a 25-year-old program
- Creators of a profession
- Educators
- Entertainers
- The nation's research resource in crime and justice
- The fastest growing industry
- The wave of the future
- The conscience of the nation
- Potential scapegoats
- The new bridge to the world (p. 1).

Of the ten, there is definitely agreement with Dr. Adler that: "One of our paramount tasks is that of being educators" (p. 3). As educators, the focus must be on continuing to strengthen the field, in the classroom and out. This will mean following the path of criminologists who have long recruited and educated individuals who would occupy old and new education vacancies. These individuals will need both practical knowledge and experience and a strong academic curriculum. Traditional criminologists continue to rely only on the academics with little use for the practical. It is put forth here that modern and future criminologists will have practical experience and knowledge similar to that of their justician counterparts.

Overall, from an academic-discipline perspective, there is more room for comparison than for contrast. Both disciplines tend to support the scientific method and are interested in criminal behavior. However, where they differ is with which aspects of that criminal behavior they address. Furthermore, at least at the undergraduate level, there seem to be more similarities than differences with regard to program missions and/or objectives and required coursework. Therefore, where else might criminal justice and criminology really differ? An examination from the perspectives of both research and practical application may provide answers. Although this will receive greater coverage in the next chapter, a brief inquiry at this time is useful.

Research

Simply based on their definitions, criminal justice and criminology are touted to use a scientific approach, which means employing the previously noted methods of data collection. Both sides support strong research efforts and are successful in obtaining funding. Both support a variety of scholarly journals where results of research can be reported. Unfortunately, there is more in the way of contrast than comparisons.

Where they differ is in what they study and why. Furthermore, how they study differs. Criminology has long been known for its strong quantitative approach (considered more scientific) to research, while criminal justice has been pseudoquantitative at best, with a leaning more strongly toward qualitative research. *Qualitative* refers to the quality: what, how, when, and where; *quantitative* refers to numbers or quantity. This difference is a growing area of contention between criminologists and justicians, where criminologists continue to argue that for criminal justice to become more accepted as a social science, the research must become more strongly quantitative. Some argue that there is little distinction between either and that both are necessary and applicable to both fields (Berg, 1995).

In response to the criticism, criminal justice researchers are becoming more strongly quantitative, and it is beginning in the criminal justice curriculums that it was a rarity for a student to be required to take a research methods or a statistics course. More recently, there appears to be a growing trend toward requiring students to take both (as is the situation in the five programs examined). Furthermore, this is occurring at both the undergraduate and graduate levels. In sum, despite the contrasts, both criminology and criminal justice support a research component.

Practical Applications

Finally, strictly from a definitional perspective, it is difficult to determine the comparisons and contrasts of the practical applications of both disciplines. Although, within its definition, criminal justice refers to practical applications, criminology also has it practical side, which will be discussed in the next chapter.

Obviously, there are many differences and similarities between criminology and criminal justice. It is contended that there are more similarities than differences. Others would argue otherwise. Regardless of which side is chosen, the reality is that criminology and criminal justice would be more successful as both social foci and academic disciplines if a greater cooperation and intertwining occurred beyond that which naturally occurs. As Pelfrey (1980) suggested:

> The discipline of criminal justice is viewed by some as being totally separate from the study of criminology. Others view the former as being an integral aspect of the latter. Criminal Justice is seen by some as applied criminology, and for others it is an area for academic concern on the part criminologists. Whether the two areas—criminal justice and criminology—are seen as one discipline or two mutually exclusive disciplines, none can rebut the fact that the two are closely intertwined. (p. 52)

It has been suggested on several occasions that the foundation of both criminology and criminal justice is crime and criminal behavior. This is similar to Pelfrey's belief that: "The main difference in the two approaches seems to be the usage of and emphasis upon the law" (p. 53). He surmises, "Where criminology uses the law as tool to define its area of interest, criminal justice is formed and defined by the criminal law" (p. 53). Since it is the law that defines those actions that are identified as criminal behaviors, the two ideas offered may be more a difference of semantics, than a true difference. Either way, the root causes require intertwinement.

The Social Focus

For justicians to adequately and effectively do their jobs—that is, to prevent and/or control criminal behavior—they must have a better understanding of why individuals commit this behavior. Since their positions do not allow them the time and resources to explore the behavior, they must rely on criminologists to proffer explanations. If there were no justicians to take forth the theories and explanations and incorporate them into programs or actions, criminologists would have little utility. As a result, for a better functioning CJS, it takes both justicians and criminologists.

The Academics

Having been educated as a criminologist, worked as a practitioner, and currently teaching as a justician, this author has been hard-pressed to recognize a big difference between the academic disciplines of criminology and criminal justice. In many cases, there appears to be very little difference in the requirements or contents of the curriculum, be it undergraduate or graduate levels (as demonstrated earlier in this chapter). Although the same thing could not have been said 25 to 30 years ago, today's curriculums are heavily intertwined, beginning with the Introduction to Criminal Justice course's section on criminology. Furthermore, it is becoming more common for introductory criminology books to have sections on the different components of the CJS. In addition to the introductory courses that are beginning to resemble each other in content but not yet in name, it is common for students in both disciplines to take more courses that discuss the CJS and its components in-depth, and on law and procedure, than in theory. There had long been a major divide in that criminal justice students seldom had to take a research and/or methods course, whereas it was a requirement for criminology students. However, this, too, is changing. During the past 10 years the trend appears to be toward requiring criminal justice students to take research methods and statistics courses, as well.

Finally, in support of intertwining, nowhere is it probably more obvious than in the memberships of the two major academic organizations: the American Society of Criminology and the Academy of Criminal Justice Sciences. A review of the membership directories finds many of the same people listed. This is reinforced if you attend both conferences where you'll see many of the same people.

Contrary to what purists of both disciplines might want to believe, for both criminology and criminal justice to persevere in the social and academic arenas, an understanding and acceptance of the two as similar, intertwining concepts that rely on each other to survive is necessary. Otherwise, both sides will continue to do battle against each other when there really is not any need. Instead, they should combine their efforts to battle the real enemy: crime and criminal behavior.

CONCLUSION

Regardless of which discipline one subscribes to, there are similarities and differences. Both are interested in understanding and controlling criminal behavior, having evolved for that purpose. As social foci, concentration by both is on understanding and dealing with criminal behavior. The criminologist would like to be able to explain why it happens so that the justician can figure out how to make sure it does not happen again.

Academically, both support a scientific approach and are interested in preparing students for graduate work or employment in the CJS. However, their approaches to each may differ. Criminology prefers a more theoretical approach while criminal justice is still more practical oriented but is moving more toward the theoretical side daily.

Either way, the similarities and differences make each discipline important to the other. Their intertwining is the key to both of their existences. The reality is, without one there is no need for the other. They are distinctively unique and must be given proper recognition as separate concepts, yet they must also be accepted for their need to intertwine. This will be enhanced in the next chapter.

FOR THE CRITICAL THINKER

1. Although crime is the root of both criminology and criminal justice as social foci, there is a difference as to how it is approached. Is this difference truly necessary? Why?

2. Reexamining criminology and criminal justice as social foci, what comparisons or contrasts, if any, are missing? How important are they to understanding the two ideals?

3. Academically, at first glance, there would seem to be a tremendous difference between criminology and criminal justice. On the other hand, closer scrutiny finds great similarities. Explain why such a difference in perspectives exists. Can they be changed?

4. Accepting that the five programs reviewed in the chapter are representative of all criminology and criminal justice programs, what are the implications? Is it possible that criminology and criminal justice could be combined into a single discipline?

5. The conclusions of this chapter tend to indicate that there are more similarities than differences between criminology and criminal justice as social foci and academic disciplines. It basically calls for the acceptance of intertwinement. How would you argue against this stance?

6

Research and Practical Applications

The two key characteristics of both criminology and criminal justice, as previously identified, are the social focus that revolves around criminal behavior and the academic, which requires using a scientific approach. It should be quite evident how criminal behavior fits, and some attention has been given to the scientific approach. Still, to fully grasp the utility of both concepts, especially as academic disciplines, further exploration in the research and applied aspects is prudent. Therefore, this chapter demonstrates, through examples, the kinds of research that are being conducted in both disciplines and how that research can be applied or be used as a practical application.

RESEARCH

Before focusing in on specific examples, what is meant by the term *research* should be explained. Although there are many formal definitions, for the purpose of this chapter the following is appropriate: Research is the investigation into or of a specifically identified phenomenon. This applies to readily recognizable and yet-to-be discovered phenomena. You will note that no specific method is mentioned. That is because research can include a multitude of scientific methods, which you should recall from the previous chapter were identified as survey, observation, life or case, and record.

Survey Research

One of the most often employed methods of research for both disciplines is the use of surveys, either self-administered or as interviews. This approach allows the obtainment of data directly from the targeted source(s). For example, in criminal justice, to further discover the extent of victimization beyond that reported to law enforcement agencies, researchers use the national victimization survey. This survey requests respondents to report the actual number of times they have been victimized and to identify the type and/or degree of victimization. Another example of criminal justice survey research is job satisfaction surveys of police, probation, and correctional officers. This type of research offers justicians better insight into areas that are too difficult to observe.

In criminology, a popular survey research item is self-reported crime studies. With these, criminologists attempt to gain a better understanding and perspective of juvenile criminality by asking high school students to complete surveys indicating the types of criminal (delinquent) behavior they have participated in without getting caught.

Although survey research is applicable to both disciplines, criminal justice appears to make more use of it than criminology. This does not mean criminologists will not take advantage of this method when necessary.

Observational Studies

While more popular among criminologists, observational studies are those where researchers gather data through firsthand observing of their targets. For example, consider how many of the sociocriminological theories center around gangs. If a criminologist wanted to continue to learn more about gang membership and activities, he or she might try "running" with a gang as a participant-observer. Through this method the researcher would experience firsthand the attraction and power of gangs. Another observational study might involve spending time at a correctional facility watching how inmates interact, to better understand prison socialization.

A justician might observe sentencing hearings in a specific drug court to attempt to determine whether there are specific patterns present that relate to the degree of sentence delivered. Perhaps a justician might ride along with a police officer to learn more about police-nonpolice interactions.

In either case, observational studies may present a more hazardous approach to research. However, from a criminological perspective it may be one of the best ways to truly learn about criminal behavior.

Life Histories or Case Studies

Probably one of the simplest methods of research for both the criminologist and the justician is through life histories or case studies— the review and analysis of documents. With respect to criminal justice, this type of research might focus on the examination of burglaries believed to be part of a series in an attempt to discover particular patterns for apprehension and future prevention. A criminologist who is interested in violent behavior might investigate the lives of a serial murderer or rapist to try to better understand why the person acted as he or she did. It may even assist in finding a means of treating this person. Again, this method might be more attractive to the criminologist than the justician.

Record Studies

The last form of scientific methodology is the use of records where the researcher evaluates and analyzes official records for relevant data. In criminology, reviewing the arrest records of a career criminal to perhaps determine if a pattern existed and what may have influenced the continuing criminality is one example. For criminal justice, analyzing crime reports for a given jurisdiction to discover the impact or influence on crime using a specific type of prevention method, such as foot patrol, is just one example, too. This method of research appears more popular in criminal justice than in criminology.

Obviously, these four methods of research provide ample options to criminologists and justicians. However, the method used will depend on the nature of the phenomenon being studied. This will become apparent in the following discussions, which use examples of research published in two mainstream journals: *Criminology* and the *Journal of Criminal Justice.*

CRIMINOLOGY

With the main interest of criminology being why individuals commit crime, it should not be surprising that research focuses on the related behavior. Thus, because crimes are extensive, so are the related behaviors, leaving broad criminological research opportunities. Additionally, trying to understand crime from a theoretical perspective and to understand the theories of criminal behavior further broaden the research opportunities. While the following are merely the tip of the research iceberg, they do well in demonstrating the diversity of criminological research.[1]

Regarding violence, Felson and Messner (1996) explored the notion of lethal intent in order to understand the outcomes

---

[1.] Although not limited to one publication in which criminological research is published, the examples provided were chosen from the journal *Criminology,* a publication of the American Society of Criminology, which has been identified as one of the top criminological journals. All the examples come from the 1995 and 1996 volumes in an effort to be as timely as possible (at least as of the writing of this text). Furthermore, the selected pieces should not be considered as better than others printed in the same volumes, but simply as representing a particular type of research effort.

of injurious attacks. They suggested that "assailants sometimes kill rather than merely injure victims to avoid either retaliation or criminal prosecution" (p. 519). Using a multiple logistic regression analysis on a data set containing information on homicides, rapes, robberies, and "pure assault" (p. 519), their findings tended to be "largely consistent with theoretical expectations" (p. 519).

It seems that the majority of research conducted tends to focus on theory: defined, utility, and applications. Brezina (1996) explored "the ways that delinquency may enable adolescents to cope with strain" (p. 39). This was done using cross-sectional and longitudinal analyses of data from the Youth in Transition survey. The results are said to be consistent with the views offered by strain theory. Reed and Yeager (1996) examined and critiqued Gottfredson and Hirschi's general theory of crime, "with particular respect to its applicability to organizational offending" (p. 357). It was their contention that Gottfredson and Hirschi's theory was too limiting. They suggested that an acceptable theory of organizational offending must consider matters of definition(s), counting the phenomena of interest, the nature of the interest, and the role of opportunity. They conclude that this theory would differ considerably from Gottfredson and Hirschi's theory of crime.

Chamlin and Cochran (1995) assessed Messner and Rosenfeld's institutional anomie theory, which suggests that "the effects of economic conditions on profit-related crime depend on the strength of noneconomic institutions" (p. 411). To complete their task, Chamlin and Cochran used cross-sectional 1980 data from all 50 states. Their findings indicated that there was indirect support for Messner and Rosenfeld's theory, "revealing that the effects of poverty on property crime depend on levels of structural indicators of the capacity of noneconomic institutions to ameliorate the criminogenic impact of economic deprivation" (p. 411).

Other examples of theory-oriented research include: Ogle, Maier-Katkin, and Bernard's (1995) discussion of the theory of homicidal behavior among women and Bueno de Mesquita and Cohen's (1995) examination of game theory, where they attempt to "answer questions about how individuals with different proclivities to use crime to accomplish ends, and different beliefs about society's fairness, are derived from strain and neoclassical deterrence theories" (p. 483).

Violence and theory are both popular arenas for research, but so are the correlates or influences on criminality. For example, Fowles and Merva (1996) sought evidence of "links between changes in distribution of wage income and criminal activity" (p. 163) finding some links to violent crimes but no links to robbery and burglary.

Harer and Steffensmeier (1996) tested for "racial difference in both violent and alcohol/drug misconduct" (p. 323) within the prison setting, concluding that blacks were more prone to violence while whites had a higher propensity toward alcohol and drug misconduct—a finding they indicated as being similar to that found in society. Simpson and Elis (1995) considered the link between gender and racial oppression as "moderating etiological variables in the study of crime" (p. 47). Employing self-reported data of a sample of 4578 juveniles extracted from the 1978 National Longitudinal Survey of Youth, their findings indicated that gender and race were influential on property and violent delinquency by modifying the effects of the independent variables.

Evans, Cullen, Dunaway, and Burton (1995) revisited the effect of religion on crime. Results from a self-reported survey of 555 individuals (over 18 years of age) indicated that "participation in religious activities was a persistent and noncontingent inhibiter of adult crime" (p. 195).

Lastly, there is a whole potpourri of criminological research possible. For example, Warr (1996) using data from the National Survey of Youth examined delinquent groups, "with special attention to the identity and role of instigators in those groups" (p. 11). Maher and Daly (1996) explored the role of women in the sale of drugs. They used an ethnographic study of women drug users from a neighborhood in New York, finding that the crack cocaine market has not provided much in the way of opportunity for women to deal drugs. Ulmer and Kramer (1996), using statistical and qualitative data from Pennsylvania, examined the extralegal differences in sentencing outcomes and whether "substantive rational sentencing criteria are intertwined with defendants' exercise of their right to trial and their race and gender" (p. 383).

Recidivism appeared to be a popular research topic. Joo, Ekland-Olson, and Kelly (1995) examined recidivism among paroled property offenders. MacKenzie, Brame, McDowall, and Souryal (1995) explored the relationship between boot camps and recidivism.

Additional examples of other research include: the impact of enhanced prison terms for felonies committed with guns (Marvell and Moody, 1995); the relationship between maltreatment as a child and delinquency (Smith and Thornberry, 1995); and Agnew's (1995) exploration of determinism, indeterminism, and crime.

One should observe from the previous discussion that criminological research is far from limited. Within the realm of criminology as a discipline, the research is often befitting the nature of the subject—that is, having strong theoretical implications. But what of its practical applications? For the criminology student, this is often not as big a concern because application is what others (justicians) do. However, the justician, as a more practical-oriented individual, may not recognize or understand how this research, particularly the strong theory-based research, is germane to what they do. Yet it is. Therefore, how would one go about demonstrating how criminological research fits into criminal justice?

Criminology Using Practical Examples

While every instructor has his or her own method for presenting material, I suggest using realistic examples to support and illustrate the subject being taught. Fortunately, this appears to be a method others advocate, too. For example, Reichel (1982) promotes the use of a 30-item checklist in which students gauge their own involvement in undetected (by law enforcement) criminal activity. Through its use, he is able to demonstrate to students that "criminal behavior is the study of our own behavior, and the criminal is the person sitting next to us in class or looking back at us from the mirror" (p. 94). Although this method may help students assess their own criminality, it doesn't appear to be very useful for explaining criminological theories.

An example of a method that *does* appear to be more advantageous to teaching criminological theories is the use of case histories. Quinn, Holman, and Tobolowsky (1992) note that the use of the case-study method helps "to bring criminological theories to life for undergraduate students at the micro level, where they are initially most comfortable" (p. 55). While there is agreement with this position and it serves well in a criminology course, it is difficult to find the time to properly use this method in the portion of the introduction to criminal justice course allocated to this subject. Therefore, one can attempt to use a condensed version of the case-study method by selecting events and information from today's news sources and current research that appear to best represent or demonstrate a particular theory or group of theories.

For example, beginning with the biological theories, one might discuss the research dealing with the examination of the brains of homosexual males (early findings indicate that these males have a smaller hypothalamus than heterosexual males), the growing acceptance of the "PMS defense," and studies linking genes to aggressive behavior. Regarding the psychological theories, discussions might include such cases as Charles Manson, Ted Bundy, John Wayne Gacy, and Jeffrey Dahmer. The cases of shootings that have occurred in workplaces or restaurants, such as post offices and McDonald's, also make good material for the application of psychological theories. Finally, with respect to the sociological theories, the best examples tend to include gang activities. These are particularly relevant since several of the theories in this group were formulated based on the study of male youths and gang activity. Another interesting aspect to discuss is the relationship of fraternities and sororities and the application of sociological theories to behaviors associated with these groups.

Applying theory to the practical world is not as difficult as it may first appear. The same holds true for other criminological research. One must simply use a similar method of application as that used with theories to the other types of research. For example, returning to a few previous examples, we might take the findings of Harer and Steffensmeier (1996) (race and prison violence) as a means to improving the environment of the prison setting by attempting to provide black inmates with means of controlling anger and violence while offering whites treatment and alternatives to drugs and alcohol. Using Maher and Daly's (1996) (women and drug sales) results as a foundation for establishing drug programs directly geared toward women might be another way to apply research results. Finally, Felson and Messner's research (1996) (lethal outcomes in injurious attacks) may assist in establishing crime prevention techniques and information valuable to the prospective victim.

The bottom line is, regardless of what the research finds, criminological research offers myriad arenas that have both purely theoretical and applied possibilities. As such, it should not simply dwindle between the covers of a journal, but should be used in whatever way it can to assist criminal justice—the social focus—to understand and deal with criminal behavior. This allows criminal justice research to focus on other aspects of the CJS.

CRIMINAL JUSTICE

By its very nature, criminal justice research is applied and often has strong practical implications. That is not to say that some of the research does not lean more toward the criminological realm and have limited practical implications. Furthermore, criminal justice-designated research is a double-edged sword, generally conducted using scientific methodologies but focusing on the applied elements of the CJS, thus creating the aura of practical application and limiting its "research" status. However, having been educated in the criminological arena, but having worked as a criminal justice practitioner, I know that there is often a certain bias toward criminal justice research as having more readily usable, practical outcomes for CJS, a goal that both criminological and criminal justice research should attain. Thus lies the basis for a more in-depth look at criminal justice research.

Like criminological research, criminal justice research is found to represent myriad topics. For the purpose at hand, the research offered easily fits under one of four main categories: police, courts, corrections, and other.[2]

Police

Probably one of the most popular areas of criminal justice research is the police, especially the law enforcement element. The reason for this is because of it being one of the most visible components of the CJS. Whether through personal contact or observation or through media reporting or portrayals, policing has become a veritable target of criticism, debate, and research. Furthermore, because of the wide variety of tasks and roles associated with policing, it provides researchers with a plethora of possibilities.

One of the more publicized incidents involving police officers is the use of force, making it an obvious target for research. Kerstetter, Rasinski, and Heiert (1996) examined allegations of exces-

---

[2.]   As with the examples of the criminology research, the criminal justice examples are all taken from the 1996 volumes of a mainstream publication, *Journal of Criminal Justice*. Again, this does not indicate that these are the best examples of research conducted in the field, just that they were readily available, current, and adequately fulfill the aim of this section.

sive use of nondeadly force by Chicago police officers to ascertain "the role of race and other factors in the disposition of complaints against police" (p. 1). To accomplish this task, they used models from social psychology applied to a random sample of cases stratified by disposition from a list of 1914 complaints filed in 1985 against Chicago police officers. Although they found that evidence and duty status were significant in the models, the "only significant racial effect in any of the models is the interactive variable reflecting the race of the investigator and the race of the complainant" (p. 1).

Although all occupations may be stressful to a degree, policing has often been identified as one of the most stressful occupations around. Storch and Panzarella (1996) studied police stress among 79 officers from three different police departments. They used a standardized measure of stress and a questionnaire about job stressors, individual job and career variables, and personal variables. They found that "more stress was experienced by officers who were inclined to think more frequently about the possibility of being injured and by officers adapting to changes in their work or family" (p. 99).

When a job involves the numerous situations and incidents that policing does, chances that an officer will be injured are great. Brandl (1996) provided a descriptive analysis of police assaults and accidents. This was accomplished through the analysis of over 2000 officer injury reports from a large midwestern police agency. A major finding was that an overwhelming majority of incidents resulted from accidents, with the second largest number of incidents resulting during the controlling or arresting of an individual.

Affirmative action has been a hotly debated topic in recent years. Its effect has not escaped policing. Stokes and Scott (1996) examined affirmative action and race norming with respect to policing. This study also looked at minority group representation in 19 municipal police departments. Its findings suggested that affirmative action has helped to increase the number of minority group members becoming police officers but that it has not had the desired affect of making departments more representative of their jurisdiction's populations.

Finally, in the past few years, domestic violence has moved to the forefront of concerns, especially police officers' responses to such situations. As a result, many states have enacted laws that require police officers to make arrests, leaving little room for discretion. Feder (1996) explored the police handling of domestic calls in Florida after the enactment of such a law. In particular, she was interested in how important the offender's presence at the scene was in influencing an arrest. This study was completed using police records for a 17-day period in 1992, which included 128 incidents meeting the research criteria. The outcome was that the offender's presence was the most powerful predictor of an arrest.

The previous examples barely skim the surface of the research focusing on the police. However, they do show the diversity of topics and methods used. Furthermore, they all support a form of scientific methodology and have practical implications.

Courts

Contrary to popular belief, the court component of the CJS offers an extremely interesting and rich choice of research topics ranging from decisions to prosecute through the appeals of verdicts and sentences. This can result in research with little to far-reaching implications. For example, the influence of race on prosecution and sentencing has long been a bone of contention among believers of a racial bias. To address that subject, in a study of 1379 cases of persons arrested and charged with a single drug felony in Sacramento County, California, Barnes and Kingsnorth (1996) found that (a) cases against African Americans were rejected or dismissed more so than those against Caucasians or Latinos, (b) Caucasians were placed on diversion or had charges reduced to misdemeanors, (c) African Americans received prison terms more often than Latinos, who received them more often than Caucasians; and (d) when sentenced to prison, African Americans and Latinos usually received longer sentences. They concluded:

> The character of inner city drug markets, coupled with law enforcement drug suppression strategies, means that African Americans and, secondarily, Latinos are more frequently charged with more severe offenses than Caucasians. These factors, rather than racial/ethnic status per se, account for the differences in the outcomes noted above. (p. 39)

It is more common to see sentencing research where race, in particular African Americans, is the main focus, but it is not the only ethnic or racial concern. Alvarez and Bachman (1996) looked at the disparity in sentence lengths received by Native Americans versus Caucasians in Arizona. After controlling for prior felony record and other demographics, the only crimes in which Native American were found to have received longer sentences than Caucasians convicted of the same crimes were robbery and burglary.

Generally, when one thinks of the courts, the first thought might be of trials. Yet trials are rare, at least proportionately to the number of people arrested and convicted. Still, trials and their associated characteristics can provide an interesting research arena, especially with respect to juries. For example, Fukurai (1996) investigated "whether jurors' social class status is equally as important as jurors' racial and ethnic characteristics in explaining disproportionate representation on jury panels" (p. 71). The findings indicated that a juror's social class is an important determinant of jury participation. Another approach was found in Levine (1996), who defended the use of the case-study method to conduct jury research. He identified both the weaknesses and strengths for use of this methodology.

Despite its constant pairing with parole, probation is actually an element of the courts and another arena for research. This is demonstrated with a study by Schneider, Ervin, and Snyder-Joy (1996), who examined the process implementation and the role of risk/need assessment instruments in supervision decisions made by probation officers. Their findings showed that the instruments were viewed negatively, at best neutrally.

As with policing, the research possibilities regarding the courts are broad. However, it appears—at least among the research articles published in the 1996 volume of the *Journal of Criminal Justice*—that policing and corrections are more popular research arenas.

Corrections

The correctional field encompasses prisons, jails, and parole. Thus, it is not surprising that there is research in all three areas. Vaughn (1996) assessed civil liability cases brought against prison officials, under Title 42 USC Section 1983, for inmate versus inmate assault. He concludes: "Comprehensive breakdowns in prison management lead to disorganization that fosters an environment in which inmate-against-inmate assaults flourish" (p. 139).

Staying with prisoners' rights as a research interest, Lee (1996) discussed prisoners' rights to recreation. He concluded that despite the many court rulings on prisoners' rights to access to recreation, "a coherent and comprehensive policy in this area has yet to emerge" (p. 167).

Remaining in the prison research venue, Jackson and Ammen (1996) explored how race might effect a correctional officer's attitude toward treatment programs. Relying on data from the Texas prison system, they found that attitude does differ, and is significantly related, based on the officer's race. Over time, African American officers became less punitive than Caucasian officers. Another research effort focusing on correctional officers was undertaken by Triplett, Mullings, and Scarborough (1996), who examined work-related stress and coping. Their research used self-reported data from a sample of correctional officers at one medium security prison. The results revealed: "Correctional officers experience many of the same organizational level stressors as those identified within the broader occupational literature, as well as those unique to their profession" (p. 291).

For decades, a mainstream perspective of the utility of prisons has been to rehabilitate. This has presented justicians with another interesting research field. Kolstad (1996) explored what offenders believed about the rehabilitative effect of imprisonment. In general, the belief was that imprisonment in and of itself was not rehabilitative and proposed that community work was more appropriate and effective with respect to being rehabilitative.

While the majority of research tends to be prison oriented, jails are not left out. For example, Stohr, Lovrich, and Wood (1996) examined whether there was a difference by gender among jail personnel with respect to training preferences (service versus security). Using data drawn from six jails, their findings indicated that there was no attitudinal difference by gender.

Finally, there appears to be a growing trend toward new or innovative means for punishing individuals. One of the more recent means is boot camps. Benda, Toombs, and Whiteside (1996) addressed recidivism among boot camp graduates, in particular, comparing drug offenders to other offenders. The study included 792 graduates of an Arkansas boot camp. The results indicated that there was not much variance in recidivism between the two groups.

Considering the previous examples, there is obviously much potential for correctional related research. Actually, it is quite clear that the research potential among all three CJS components is abundant. Still, the research that easily falls within the confines of "other" may outweigh (strictly by volume) the research in and among all three components combined.

Other

Because *other* can be defined as anything that doesn't specifically fall under police, courts, and corrections, some might figure that this may not leave much of an arena for research. That presumption would be wrong. The possibilities—crime, juveniles, laws, and health issues such as AIDS and violence—are enormous. The forthcoming examples merely scratch the surface.

AIDS

With the publicity and notoriety that AIDS has received, it was only a matter of time before it would be included in criminal justice research. Lanier and Gates (1996) measured the influence of the AIDS Risk Reduction Model (ARRM) on high-risk adolescents' knowledge, attitudes, and self-reported behavior. Analyzing data collected from 393 incarcerated juveniles, they found, "The ARRM is effective for understanding the factors that influence AIDS risk avoidance" (p. 537).

Health and Violence

Health and violence seem to garner considerable attention, as observed by the following examples: Anderson, Grandison, and Dyson (1996) visited the issue of victims of random violence and the public health implications; Madriz (1996) examined the perceptions of risk in the workplace; and Johnson and Sigler (1996) explored public perceptions of interpersonal violence.

Fear of Crime

The fear of crime, especially by the elderly, is an interesting research topic. McCoy, Wooldredge, Cullen, Dubeck, and Browning (1996) surveyed 1448 elderly residents of Dade County, Florida, in an attempt to assess the impact of fear of crime based on status characteristics, victimization experience, and other measures of life situations. The findings prompted four conclusions:

1. The elderly did not appear to have high levels of fear.
2. Evidence existed that while victimization experiences increased with age, it was not a main determinant of fear.

3. Including life-situation variables helped explain the variance for fear of crime.
4. The dissatisfaction with their neighborhood and their vulnerability "were important correlates of fear of crime" (p. 191).

Legalized Gambling

The growth of legalized gambling in this country makes it inevitable that someone will recognize the research potential. Chang (1996) studied the impact that casinos have on crime in Biloxi, Mississippi. Analyzing data for 118 offenses, Chang discovered that there was no increase in crime rates during the first two years of operation but did note that in the first year there was a substantial decrease in crime, only for it to return to its precasino days levels in the second year.

Racial Influence

Lastly, as noted earlier, racial influence on various aspects of criminal justice is a relatively popular research arena. Previously mentioned was research that looked at race and jury participation and race and sentencing. Weitzer (1996) offered research findings examining the extent of racial discrimination throughout the criminal justice system—that is, by police, courts, and correctional agencies. Weitzer's methodology was to review an extensive body of literature identifying "racial effects at certain points in the criminal justice system and in certain social contexts" (p. 309). He suggested that discrimination is not as extensive as believed or anticipated. Furthermore, he noted that there was a host of methodological and analytical deficiencies in the research he evaluated, which future research needs to rectify.

In all, whether it's policing, courts, corrections, crime, law, or miscellaneous others, there is no shortage of research topics for the justician. Therefore, the ability to promote criminal justice as a social science through research is possible. Furthermore, it appears that much of the research can have direct influence on a particular aspect or portion of the CJS with much greater frequency than criminological research. It also employs various readily identifiable scientific approaches. Yet criminal justice research still does not receive the standing it so richly deserves. On the other hand, perhaps the importance of criminological research is overstated? Realistically, research in both areas is important, even more so is the meshing of the two with respect to research.

CONCLUSION

The research potential within both criminology and criminal justice is incredible. While the outcomes from both can have important ramifications and results, from a purely applicable perspective, criminal justice research is stronger. The previous chapter focused on the general intertwining of criminology and criminal justice. This is important with respect to research, too. By intertwining the two, the research potential is immeasurable. Furthermore, perhaps workable solutions could actually be discovered for controlling crime if behavioral cause and methods of control were correlated for practical purposes. For example, if research could combine gang member behavior with alternatives to gang membership, chances are good that a diversion program could be designed and implemented. You can't repair or defer something if you don't know what causes it in the first place. Research that could (a) identify the criminal behavior and what influences it and (b) identify means of addressing it would be extremely useful to the CJS. Unfortunately, as long as both sides continue to argue as to which side is better or more important, crime will continue to be a major problem, and the abundance of research with only minimal application potential will grow.

FOR THE CRITICAL THINKER

1. How important is research to criminology and criminal justice? What is the most important aspect?

2. Having reviewed the information, does it seem reasonable to claim that both criminology and criminal justice support a scientific approach through research? Which approach appears the most useful?
3. Discuss the implications of the criminological research examined in the chapter. What are the pros and cons of these research efforts?
4. Despite its natural inclination to be practical oriented, can criminal justice research be purely theoretical? If so, how would it differ from criminological research?
5. Should future research attempt to combine both a criminological and criminal justice approach? Which might be more valuable? What topics should be researched from the combined perspective?

The Future

7

If one subscribed to the popular belief in fortune tellers, seers, psychics, or prognosticators, predicting the future would be easy. However, not being one of those subscribers, I will not make an attempt to predict the future. Instead, this chapter will be a *speculation* as to what is possible for both criminology and criminal justice, as social foci and academic disciplines, in the years to come. Although there are tendencies to simply accept that "history repeats itself" and simply reiterate what has occurred, the approach here is to look at what is possible using some previously offered materials as foundations. Therefore, this chapter concludes the text by seeking out possible outcomes for criminology and criminal justice.

AS SOCIAL FOCI

Despite the distinctions offered throughout this text, there has also be the one main connecting theme: As social foci, criminology and criminal justice are concerned with criminal behavior, especially violent crime. As Roberts (1994) noted, "Violent crime is one of the most serious social problems facing American society" (p. 4). Therefore, it should be accepted that criminology will continue to focus on why criminal behavior occurs and better ways to treat those who commit crime. Criminal justice will continue to focus on controlling criminal behavior. However, in order for both of these social foci to continue to progress and to better speculate on how they might grow and/or change, a better grasp of the future of what is the root of this criminal behavior—crime—is mandatory. Therefore, some speculative views on crime are appropriate.

In 1989,[1] criminologist Georgette Bennett's revised and updated text *Crimewarps* provided thought-provoking speculations for the future of crime in America. To further speculate about the future of crime, Bennett's six crimewarps[2] will be used as the foundation.

Crimewarp I: The New Criminals

> *Traditional criminals—young, male, poor, uneducated—will increasingly be displaced by older, more upscale offenders. The number of crimes committed by women will accelerate, not only in stereotyped areas like prostitution, but in white-collar and domestic violence. Teenagers will commit fewer, but more terrible crimes. Senior citizens will enter the crime scene as geriatric delinquents.* (1989, pp. xiii–xiv)

There is little argument that the face of the criminal will continue to change from the traditional, stereotypical young,

---

[1.] Although this version was published in 1989, it should be noted that the writing and thoughts for this text actually began in the early 1980s. In many respects, it is safe to say that by the time this text is published, it will be a good 10 years after the development of Bennett's crimewarps. Therefore, speculating on the future of crime through the reviewing of her visions of the future seemed appropriate.

[2.] Bennett notes that she coined the term *crimewarp* "to describe the bends in today's trends that will affect the way we live tomorrow" (1989, p. xiii). It is a very appropriate term for speculative purposes.

poor, minority-group member males. Bennett noted that female criminality would increase, and it has—and it will continue to do so. Where future speculation may differ is in the type of criminality involving women, particularly, juvenile females.

According to a 1996 National Center for Juvenile Justice report, the arrests of female juveniles for violent crimes increased 55 percent from 1989 to 1993, contrasting with a 33 percent increase for juvenile males. Examination of FBI Uniform Crime Data from 1991 through 1995 found that the rates of female juveniles arrested rose 35 percent, almost double that of males. The two areas for which female juveniles were arrested the most were larceny-theft and aggravated assaults. Between 1993 and 1994 alone, the number of females arrested (for all crimes) who were under 18 years of age rose 13 percent. Among the index crimes, the largest growth was in arson and robbery (16 and 15 percent, respectively). For other crimes, the largest percentages of change were associated with drug violations and gambling (50 and 46 percent, respectively). In terms of white-collar crime, there was an increase of 30 percent in arrests for fraud.

Obviously, female criminality is significantly on the rise. With census figures indicating that the population is slightly over 50 percent female, one could only speculate that female criminality will continue to increase in all crime areas, not just the traditional ones. Despite the obvious trend, it should be noted that males are still consistently arrested more often than females. In 1995 among all persons arrested, 80 percent were male. What might this mean for the future? Males will continue to be the dominant criminals, but females, especially juveniles, will continue to increase their criminal activities in numbers and by percentage far greater than males.

As for the elderly, despite a nation that is getting older—in 1994, some 45 percent of the population was between the ages of 22 and 49, whereas in 1964 less than 30 percent of the population fell within this age range—criminal activity among the elderly will probably remain consistent. In 1994, among all persons arrested, 4.2 percent were over the age of 50 while representing almost one quarter of the U.S. population. This compares to the group aged 22 to 49 who comprised 51.6 percent of all those arrested. Furthermore, if you examine the arrest percentages by smaller age brackets, arrests decrease as age increases (see Table 7–1). Therefore, the future criminal still appears to part of the "under 40 crowd."

From a racial perspective, the largest percentage of those arrested have long been white. In 1994 and 1995, 66 and 67 percent of those arrested were white—not too surprising since whites still make up approximately 80 percent of the population. However, according to the 1990 census, the number of whites had decreased since 1980 (–3.1 percent) while the largest growth was among Hispanics (2.4 percent). Whether racial composition changes will affect criminality is still yet to be seen. Even though blacks made up 31 percent of those arrested in 1994, current statistics do not categorize Hispanics into a separate category. Often they are either grouped with the whites

Table 7–1. Percent Distribution of Persons Arrested, by Age, in the United States, 1994*

Age Group	Persons Arrested
Age 12 and younger	1.8
13 to 15	8.4
16 to 18	12.8
19 to 21	11.8
22 to 24	10.5
25 to 29	14.8
30 to 34	14.4
35 to 39	10.9
40 to 44	6.7
45 to 49	3.7
50 to 54	1.9
55 to 59	1.0
60 to 64	.6
Age 65 and older	.7

*Adapted from the *Sourcebook of Criminal Justice Statistics 1995* (p. 397).

and/or the blacks. So it is possible that the race of crime may take on some changes, but chances are good that it will remain relatively the same, with blacks (African Americans) still being arrested in disproportionate numbers (in 1990, African Americans were 12 percent of the U.S. population).

Implications

For criminal justice, the implications seem to be dealing with and preventing female criminality, particularly among female juveniles. For criminology, the focus will need to be on explaining why the behavior is occurring and how to best treat those who commit crimes. Furthermore, both will need to continue to address the inequities occurring in the processing of offenders. This is particularly true with respect to processing minority and nonminority juvenile offenders (McNeece, 1994).

Crimewarp II: The March of Crime

> *Crime will become freer of geography. Less of it will take place at the neighborhood level. Where crime is spatially bound, it will shift from the Northeast to the Sunbelt and into suburban and rural areas.* (1989, p. xiv)

To date, the data available definitely support this crimewarp with no remission in site. According to 1995 UCR information, regionally, the southern states accounted for 38 percent of all crime index offenses while the northeastern states accounted for 16 percent of the total. Yet by crime rate, the western states had a 6,083 (per 100,000) rate, while the northeast boasted the lowest, 4,180 crime rate. Only the West had an increased crime rate over 1994. Because it appears that more people are moving to the better weather areas of the country, it is only logical that criminality will be higher in the more populated areas. This is supported when one observes the arrest rates by city size. For example, in 1994 for 60 cities with a population of over 250,000, the arrest rate was 7824 per 100,000—the highest rate among the six-group division used. However, an interesting observation was that the second highest arrest rate took place in cities with populations of less than 10,000 (6484). The lowest crime rate was for cities with populations between 25,000 and 49,999 (5341).

The other trend for the future is the increase in suburban and rural crimes. Available data trends show that crime and arrest rates have continually risen in both areas. Again, though, this should not be too surprising, what with populations growing in both these areas.

With no immediate decreasing change in movement in sight to the South and West, to the suburbs, or to rural America, it is safe to speculate that the crimewarp will maintain its veracity and can continue to be applied to the immediate future.

Implications

If the trends continue, criminal justice will need to expand its focus and control to the more populated areas of the country. Resources will need to be redirected toward the more densely populated cities, counties, and rural environments, where for years there has not been as great a need. Criminologists will continue to ponder the effects of population density and weather as two of the social correlates to criminal behavior.

Crimewarp III: Ring Around the White Collar

> *The street crimes that scare us will decrease in relation to more impersonal, far-reaching white-collar crimes. Computers, cashless money, technological secrets will become the new booty. Patterns of consumer fraud will mold themselves around changed demographics, and we will find new ways of cheating old institutions.* (p. xiv)

What many of us fear is being a victim of violent crime, perhaps with good reason. Comparing 1985 to 1994, the number of violent crime offenses charged increased by 52 percent, with the largest increase being among motor vehicle thefts (48 percent). Yet in 1995 the number of violent crimes reported was the lowest it had been since 1989. This caps off a downward trend that has been apparent since the late 1980s. Regardless of this trend, many of us still are concerned with violent crime. Crimewarp III suggests that street crime (roughly translated as violent crime) will decrease and all-encompassing white-collar crime will increase.

Because statistics describing white-collar crimes are still relatively uncommon, it is difficult to demonstrate what has occurred since the provision of this crimewarp. As Wellford and Ingraham (1994) advised, "To date there are no acceptable estimates of the total cost of this type of crime. The U.S. Chamber of Commerce has estimated that employee theft alone accounts for 20 percent of the cost of all manufactured goods. However, this estimate is poorly constructed and obviously ignores other forms of business crimes" (p. 78). Still, there is knowledge of its occurrence.

On the other hand, anecdotal information may well lend credence to the prospect that the future of crime lies within technology, but not just for nonviolent crime. Within the past few years there have been numerous reports of individuals robbed at ATMs or lured from the safety of their homes via the computer (Internet and E-mail). This is a trend that will continue because people are becoming more dependent on easy money access and meeting others through the computer. Furthermore, the number of crimes that can be committed through electronic transfers and computer hacking will continue to rise. Therefore, although street crime may continue to decrease, crimes in general will increase just through the use of different environments and tools, such as one's home or bank and with a computer.

Implications

The most obvious implication for criminal justice is the training of those, particularly law enforcement officers, who will have to prevent, investigate, and prosecute technologically driven crimes. The implications for criminology is not as drastic in that much of what it has to offer will simply be redirected toward the techno criminal. Still, the environment is ripe for high-tech invasion. As Grau (1996) suggested,

> In general, the high-tech stage is set: 1) Cyberspace overlays a more powerfully explosive physical environment. 2) Tele-puting provides abundant opportunities for mental wrong-doings as well as crime control. 3) Remotely controlled operations provide the coverage of anonymity for the criminal as well as the means for more effective and efficient criminal justice management (p. 269).

Obviously, technology will have a tremendous impact on both criminal justice and criminology.

Crimewarp IV: The Politics of Pleasure

> *Despite a deeply rooted Puritan ethic and its contemporary expression in the New Right, some consensual crimes—drug abuse, homosexuality, prostitution, gambling—will be legalized. Others, like pornography, will be subject to stricter regulation.* (p. xiv)

Of all the crimewarps, the evidence supporting this one is probably the greatest. There is no doubt that the pursuit of pleasure, regardless of its form, is a growing requirement of many Americans. In this crimewarp, four consensual crimes are identified as change possibilities.

Beginning with **drugs,** there continues to be the conflicting drive toward sustaining from their use to legalizing them. For example, in 1996 the voters of the State of California approved legalizing the availability of marijuana for medical purposes. This opened a wide spectrum of debate as to what is considered a medical ailment worthy of this form of treatment.

The information on, openness to, and the social strength of **homosexuality** has witnessed extensive development since 1989. Most states no longer have laws against certain activities strongly related to homosexuality, such as sodomy. Other states have gone as far as recognizing the domestic partner of a gay or lesbian for insurance and other employment-related benefits. And in 1996 Hawaii became the first state to legally accept and recognize marriages between same-sex individuals. Yet despite what appears to be the growing acceptance of homosexuality, there is still a strong contingent that opposes it. For example, the federal government was contemplating a law that would allow states not to recognize Hawaiian married same-sex couples and some states, like Colorado, continue to try to create laws that would limit the recognition of homosexuality with respect to affirmative action, work benefits, and marriage. Because of the growing number and political strength of homosexuals, future speculation continues to accept the decriminalizing of related crimes.

Of the four, **prostitution** is probably the one crime for which there has been little change, and more than likely that trend will continue. Despite the moral and ethical implications of prostitution, the fear of venereal diseases and especially AIDS keeps the chances of legalizing prostitution limited. Even in Nevada where it has been legal for many years, tight reins are kept on its growth, and it is limited to only a few areas of the state.

If there is one area that this crimewarp has come the closest to predicting correctly, it is **gambling**. A multibillion dollar industry, gambling has, in the past 10 years, gone from being a one-state (Nevada) commodity to a booming national business. Most states support a lottery, and many more states are allowing the development of riverboat and land-based gambling. This follows the growth of gambling on Native American reservations. Ultimately, it appears that gambling will become a state-supported revenue generator. However, there are still those who are fighting gallantly to limit or stop what is considered a potentially dangerous personal economic hazard. Still, the trend seems to be heading toward legalization.

Finally, the restricting of **pornography** seems to be right on the mark. With the widespread availability of the Internet and the ease with which pornographic materials can be posted and accessed, it has created a new need for control. Although recent federal legislation limiting access and what could be posted is still fighting constitutional court battles, the future does require some efforts for limitations. Currently, the computer can be used to access, receive, or send pornographic materials with little chance of apprehension or punishment. The future will need to address this situation. Furthermore, as it has been suggested, how society looks at pornography may need to change, especially as it relates to violence and sex (Albanese, 1996a).

In all, the politics of pleasure does have ramifications for the future of certain criminally related activities. Already we have seen drastic changes in drug usage, gambling, and homosexuality. Those changes are not limited to these areas.

Implications

Within criminal justice, law changes and enforcement will take away some old crimes and add new ones. In particular, where gambling is concerned, this opens a whole new realm of criminal possibilities, the likes of which current law enforcement is not ready for—then again, neither is the rest of the system. The future will require study and recognition of the possible crime acts that can occur and how they must be prevented. Criminology will be faced with a new direction of study that may not actually involve criminality so much as understanding why these particular areas are so enticing to so many people.

Crimewarp V:
The Ups and Downs of Big Brother

> *Long entrenched crime-fighting strategies will be displaced by leaner, more focused, less personal tactics. Efficiency and coverage will be enhanced by the proliferation of computers and high-tech listening/detection devices. Self-help, security hardware, and private police will reduce the reliance on traditional law enforcement. New architectural designs will build crime-proofing into the environment.* (p. xiv)

When one considers all the technological advances that have already taken place, plus the ever-changing face of technology, it is not difficult to imagine what the future might hold. We have already become a series of numbers to which personal information is relatively easy to access through computers; we can already tell who's calling us without answering a phone, receive calls or messages practically anywhere we are; we are photographed or videotaped at myriad businesses; in some places we are having our thumbprints placed on our driver's license; and we can even be electronically monitored as a form of punishment. There is no doubt that the future holds a refining and strengthening of "keeping tabs" on our personal doings. Still, what effect this will have on traditional crime enforcement is yet to be known.

Bennett suggested that we will move toward leaner, more focused, less personal, tactics of crime fighting. Yet for approximately the past 10 years, many police departments have been attempting to return to a more personal approach through community policing. This strategy has become one of the most popular attempts to fight crime in decades. Thanks primarily to funding from the federal government, community policing is fast becoming the strategy of the future. Unfortunately, there are those, myself included, who are cynical and view community policing as being popular for as long as the money lasts—unless of course, we see dramatic changes in criminal behavior resulting from its implementation. Because other such attempts have been made over the years and have not been very successful at crime fighting, how effectual community policing will be or how long it will last is still up for debate.

Ultimately, how technology and new approaches to enforcement will affect criminal behavior will depend on the development of laws, constitutionality, and the amount of intrusion into our personal lives we will allow. One thing is certain, no one is ready to stop developing new means to improve society's well-being and, especially, to limit or stop criminal behavior.

Implications

The infusion of electronics and computers has already begun to affect criminal justice. The police can access information about a person through mobile data terminals in their vehicles or match fingerprints from a crime scene through a computer. Future implications include improved computer usage, which means having to better train officers. The courts and corrections will continue to take advantage of electronic monitoring to supervise and incarcerate individuals. This means more money and additional training for all those involved. A view of the future with respect to technology might best be described by Archambeault (1996):

> If the past is an indicator of the future, then it is logical to take current evolving technologies and project their usage into the future. Three emerging computer technologies have significant implications for criminal justice of the twenty-first centuries: artificial intelligence, virtual reality, and biomedical research into direct brain-computer linkage. (p. 310)

Crimewarp VI:
Paying the Tab for the Bill of Rights

> *Some of our civil liberties will be displaced in an effort to stem crime and the moral anarchy that underlies it. The erosion will occur in the process of ceding our privacy to computer files and our moral judgment to ultraconservatives.* (p. xiv)

As a nation, the United States is probably by far the best in the world when it comes to the provision of personal rights. Our Constitution, with assistance from the courts, provides a formidable tool against unnecessary government intrusions. Yet this same protector has assisted in the release of many individuals, who should have been incarcerated for committing crimes, because it was not properly used. The question for the future is whether we, as a people, are willing to forego some of those rights and liberties in the name of justice, to prevent and control criminality. Granted, we already do that in many circumstances (for example, security checks at airports, drug tests for employment, or providing personal information to obtain credit), but how far are we willing to go? Rather than speculate that we are willing to go to great lengths for the sake of justice, perhaps the future will revolve strongly around the question, How much freedom are we willing to give up in the name of justice?

Implications

The implications for both criminal justice and criminology rests upon what direction we ultimately take. Fewer liberties and constitutional freedoms might well severely increase the power of the justice system, a power we are already leery to provide. What effect that would have on criminal behavior will be an interesting avenue of study for criminology.

Closing Thoughts

The future of criminal justice and criminology as social foci are far from predictable. Much of what happens is a result of politics, interest groups, and who has the most money to force change (Muraskin and Roberts, 1996). It also depends on what tactic society will take to try to better control human behavior in general. If the many social systems that once strongly influenced our behavior (for example, education, religion, family) make a strong comeback, then there is a better chance of positive changes in criminal behavior without government forcing the issue through the CJS. However, if these same systems continue to deteriorate, then it is anyone's best guess as to the future of criminal behavior.

Then again, maybe both justicians and criminologists need to look at the mistakes that have been made in the past in order to preserve the future. For example, Albanese (1996b) suggests that the problems in contemporary criminal justice result from five fundamental mistakes:

1. The failure to consider an explanation of crimes based on ethical decision making, given the inadequacies of positivistic, classical, and structural approaches
2. The failure to devote more attention to generally poor police training and low clearance rates
3. The failure to realize that winning cases and moving caseloads have overshadowed the original purposes of truth and justice in the adjudication process
4. The failure to consider an alternative approach to corrections based on punishment *and* rehabilitation rather than punishment *or* rehabilitation
5. The failure to pay greater attention to the early lives of young people and their families, from whom much subsequent criminal behavior emerges (p. 549)

Although the preceding is just one person's view, it is this type of view or introspection that the future of criminal justice and criminology will require because of their status as important social foci. This, in turn, makes them valuable academic disciplines.

AS ACADEMIC DISCIPLINES

In 1979 Richard Myren wrote, "What the future will bring to criminal justice and criminology programs in higher education is an unknown" (p. 32). In 1997, this statement is still very relevant. However, since 1979 there have been some advances, especially in criminal justice, on which future speculation can be built.

For starters, the number of undergraduate and graduate criminal justice programs have grown and do not show signs of faltering. Best-guess estimates offer that there are approximately 100,000 students seeking criminal justice or criminology degrees, and because of the popularity as a field of study for both would-be and current employees in the CJS, there is no reason to believe this will change. Because of the growth in the number of students, the need continues for educators, preferably ones with a Ph.D. in criminal justice or criminology. This forces growth in doctoral-granting programs. However, numbers' growth is just one aspect of the future of criminal justice and criminology.

Another important element is their growth as fully accepted social science disciplines. Many would argue that this is not as much of a problem for criminology as it is for criminal justice, and they would be correct. Criminal justice will need to persist in shedding the practical or hands-on aura for the more theoretical yet applicable approach to instruction. This is probably the most difficult task because of the applied nature of criminal justice and the prospects of employment that students have in the CJS. It is imperative for the future of criminal justice as an academic discipline that it can persevere as a cross-product of theory and practicality.

On the other side, criminology will need to further establish itself as a reasonable alternative to the study of criminal justice by demonstrating its importance within the realm of criminal justice. One way this may happen is through the recognition that the study of criminological theories is not limited to sociology or criminological courses. Actually, it appears to have become a standard part of introduction to criminal justice courses. Furthermore, personal observation finds that one of the more popular reasons why non-criminal justice students take the introduction to criminal justice course is that they want to learn more about criminal behavior. What they may learn in that course may lead them toward a separate criminology course when available. The most difficult task will be to attract students interested in majoring in criminology because of the lack of job potential connected with it.

Perhaps the ultimate answer for both disciplines is to merge them into a program that Meeth (1978) describes as transdisciplinary. According to Meeth, "Whereas interdisciplinary programs start with the discipline, transdisciplinary programs start with the issue or problem and, through the processes of problem solving, bring to bear the knowledge of those disciplines that contribute to a solution or resolution" (1978, p. 10). This idea has merit with respect to criminal justice and criminology, assuming that it is accepted that the underlying problem for both is criminal behavior. Using that as a starting point, addressing it from both disciplines' perspectives would create the transdisciplinary approach and provide both with the elements needed to sustain future growth and acceptance, a strong theoretical base and an applied knowledge attractive to those interested in pursuing or already maintaining a career in the CJS.

Regardless of what is ultimately accomplished, the simple truth is that both disciplines, albeit more so criminal justice, will continue to flourish. What will be of interest in the future is just how they flourish and whether they will become more intertwined or grow further apart. It is suggested that the two look to become more intertwined. Either way, research and practical applications will remain important attributes to both.

RESEARCH AND PRACTICAL APPLICATIONS

In the previous chapter, research and practical applications of both criminal justice and criminology were explored. There should be little room for doubt as to the future of both. As long as there is crime, criminal behavior, and a system to deal with both, there will remain a need for research, especially that which has practical applications. For example, criminal justice research needs to focus on the effectiveness and efficiency of community policing, intensive probation, and determinate sentencing. Criminology research should focus on elements of society that influence criminal behavior for which society might be able to control, such as lack of education or unemployment. The study of why female criminality is increasing will be extremely relevant, especially if a controllable correlation can be found, such as abuse or issues of self-esteem. In addition, criminology has begun and will need to continue to address two long-ignored arenas: feminist criminological thought and how African American justicians and criminologists are reexamining and reassessing crime and justice to provide less culturally biased data and information about criminal behavior.

The fact is, from both fields much is being written that definitely seems to provide an indication of future research and thought. This can be seen just by examining new books being published in the field. The following are examples of new 1997 titles from Sage Publishing,[3] designated as criminology books, that should help indicate where current thought and research is and where it may be going:

- *The Problem of Crime* (Edited by J. Muncie and E. McLaughlin) is described as a text that examines conceptual and definitional issues regarding crime and deviance. It looks at the diversity and history of crime as well as the political ramifications.
- *Criminological Perspectives* (Edited by Muncie, McLaughlin, and M. Langan) is a text that reflects and represents diverse theoretical inquiry regarding criminology. It begins with the origins of criminology and ends with looking at what is within and beyond criminology.
- *Racism and Criminology* (Edited by D. Cook and B. Hudson) is a critique of the existing empirical research on race and criminal justice. It also presents advances in criminological and sociological theories.
- *Imagining Crime* (A. Young) explores how criminology, criminal law, the media, and ordinary everyday experiences are used to solve the crime problem. Furthermore, it discusses criminology's resistance to several aspects, such as feminist intervention.

[3.]   There are a number of publishing companies that provide a plethora of books in criminology and criminal justice. Sage was chosen because it tends to be among the most prolific at publishing titles that are more topically oriented and not geared as the "know-all" introductory-type texts offered by others.

Obviously, theoretical approaches and explorations are still very attractive to research and publishing. The previous titles definitely support that there is, and will continue to be, an interest in the theoretical approach to explaining criminality. More of the same should be expected in the future.

Criminal justice being so much broader in scope and nature, its possible works are extensive. Here are just a few to help demonstrate where research might be heading:

- *Americans View Crime and Justice* (Edited by T. Flanagan and D. Longmire) reports the analysis of a recent National Crime and Justice Survey (conducted in June 1995). Responses from 1000 adults on a variety of issues, such as gun control and capital punishment, are analyzed and interpreted as to the opinions of these individuals as a representation of how Americans view crime.
- *Three Strikes and You're Out* (Edited by D. Shichor and D. Sechrest) examines the influence and effect of legislation effective in 16 states through a diverse yet focused collection of writings. The 12 chapters are divided among four areas: legal and historical issues, implementing the law, system impacts, and special issues.
- *Choosing Correctional Options That Work* (Edited by A. Harland) details a much needed view into correctional options. It also examines what works through in-depth examinations of theory and empirical data.

In addition to the above, several new works were available that look at drugs, juveniles, family violence, and sexual assaults on college campuses.

It is quite evident just from one publishing company the plethora of research and writings being offered to explain and explore criminological and criminal justice issues. When the prospects are multiplied by the large number of publishers of works in either area, it is clear that the future of both is solid. Still, regardless of the fact that there is much published and more to come, ultimately the research must have strong practical applications or it will be of little value. Therefore, the future of both should be to concentrate on that which is relevant, pertinent, and practical.

CONCLUSION

To try to predict the future of anything is ludicrous, even more so of something that is still relatively unstable and easily changeable like criminal justice and criminology. However, some speculation can be offered. As social foci, both will continue to grow, change, challenge, and receive respect. As long as there is a need to control certain types of behavior, especially criminal behavior, there will be a need for criminal justice, which, in turn, provides a need for criminology.

With the existence of both as social foci, the need continues for both as academic disciplines—one to study the processes and the other the reasons for the processes. Both lead to research and practical applications in which to improve the CJS and the behavior of those who make it necessary to have a CJS.

Whatever the future holds, it will be interesting. For those employed in the CJS, studying either criminal justice or criminology, or conducting research with an eye on applicable findings, the future appears to be wide open, full of opportunities. Let us make the best of them.

FOR THE CRITICAL THINKER

1. Reviewing the crimewarps, what appears to be missing for future concerns? Which one of the crimewarps discussed may have the most relevance for the future of both criminology and criminal justice?
2. Based on the crimewarps, what do you see as the future of both criminology and criminal justice as social foci? Is crime the core to the future of both? If so, how might be the best way to address it?
3. Academically, there is the link between criminology and criminal justice. What is the future of that link? Can

the two become better linked or intertwined? How might this influence the future of both?

4. Undoubtedly, there is and will continue to be a plethora of possible research topics. What should be the focus of future research? Should criminology and criminal justice research efforts be combined?

5. Considering the content of this text, and the author's obvious support of combining the two disciplines, what position would you take: maintaining a separation of the two disciplines or pushing for greater intertwinement? Why?

References

Adler, F. 1995. "Who Are We? A Self-analysis of Criminal Justice Specialists." *ACJS Today, 14*(1):1, 3, 21, 26.

Agnew, R. 1995. "Determinism, Indeterminism, and Crime: An Empirical Exploration." *Criminology, 33*(1):83–110.

Albanese, J. S. 1996a. "Looking for a New Approach to the Old Problem: The Future of Obscenity and Pornography." In *Visions for Change: Crime and Justice in the Twenty-first Century*, R. Muraskin and A. R. Roberts, eds. Upper Saddle River, NJ: Prentice Hall, 60–72.

Albanese, J. S. 1996b. Presidential Address: "Five Fundamental Mistakes of Criminal Justice." *Justice Quarterly, 13*(4):549–565.

Alvarez, A., and R. D. Bachman. 1996. "American Indians and Sentencing Disparity: An Arizona Test." *Journal of Criminal Justice, 24*(6):549–561.

Anderson, J. F., T. Grandison, and L. Dyson. 1996. "Victims of Random Violence and the Public Health Implication: A Health Care or Criminal Justice Issue?" *Journal of Criminal Justice, 24*(5):379–392.

Archambeault, W. G. 1996. "Impact of Computer Based Technologies on Criminal Justice: Transition to the Twenty-first Century." In

Visions for Change: Crime and Justice in the Twenty-first Century, R. Muraskin and A. R. Roberts, eds. Upper Saddle River, NJ: Prentice Hall, 299–316.

Barnes, C. W., and R. Kingsnorth. 1996. "Race, Drug, and Criminal Sentencing: Hidden Effects of the Criminal Law." *Journal of Criminal Justice*, 24(1):39–56.

Beccaria, Cesare. 1963. *On Crimes and Punishment*. Henry Paolucci, trans. New York: Bobbs-Merrill.

Benda, B. B., N. J. Toombs, and L. Whiteside. 1996. "Recidivism among Boot Camp Graduates: A Comparison of Drug Offenders to Other Offenders." *Journal of Criminal Justice*, 24(3):41–254.

Bennett, G. 1989. *Crimewarps: The Future of Crime in America*. New York: Doubleday Books.

Berg, B. L. 1995. *Qualitative Research Methods for the Social Sciences*, 2d ed. Boston: Allyn and Bacon.

Brandl, S. G. 1996. "In the Line of Duty: A Descriptive Analysis of Police Assaults and Accidents." *Journal of Criminal Justice*, 24(3):255–264.

Brezina, T. 1996. "Adapting to Strain: An Examination of Delinquent Coping Responses." *Criminology*, 34(1):39–60.

Bueno de Mesquita, B., and L. E. Cohen. 1995. "Self-interest, Equity, and Crime Control: A Game-Theoretic Analysis of Criminal Decision Making." *Criminology*, 33(4):483–518.

Chamlin, M. B., and J. K. Cochran. 1995. "Assessing Messner and Rosenfeld's Institutional Anomie Theory: A Partial Test." *Criminology*, 33(3):411–430.

Champion, D. J. 1990. *Criminal Justice in the United States*. Columbus, OH: Merrill Publishing.

Chang, S. 1996. "Impact of Casinos on Crime: The Case of Biloxi, Mississippi." *Journal of Criminal Justice*, 24(5):431–436.

Conrad, John P. 1979. "Criminology and Criminal Justice: Definitions, Trends, and the Future—The First View." *Two Views of Criminology and Criminal Justice: Definitions, Trends, and the Future*. Joint Commission on Criminology and Criminal Justice Education and Standards, 7–22.

Crime in America 1995. Washington, D.C.: Federal Bureau of Investigation.

Cullen, F. 1995. "Fighting Back: Criminal Justice as an Academic Discipline." *ACJS Today* (Jan/Feb):1, 3.

Dantzker, M. L. 1995. *Understanding Today's Police*. Boston, MA: Prentice Hall.

Evans, T. D., F. T. Cullen, R. G. Dunaway, and V. S. Burton, Jr. 1995. "Religion and Crime Reexamined: The Impact of Religion, Secular Controls, and Social Ecology on Adult Criminality." *Criminology*, 33(2):195–224.

Feder, L. 1996. "Police Handling of Domestic Calls: The Importance of Offender's Presence in the Arrest Decision." *Journal of Criminal Justice*, 24(6):481–490.

Felson, R. B., and S. F. Messner. 1996. "To Kill or Not to Kill? Lethal Outcomes in Injurious Attacks." *Criminology*, 34(4):519–545.

Female Offenders in the Juvenile Justice System: Statistics Summary. 1996. Rockville, MD: Juvenile Justice Clearinghouse.

Fowles, R., and M. Merva. 1996. "Wage Inequality and Criminal Activity: An Extreme Bounds Analysis for the United States, 1975–1990." *Criminology*, 34(2):163–182.

Fukurai, Hiroshi. 1996. "Race, Social Class, and Jury Participation: New Dimensions for Evaluating Discrimination in Jury Service and Jury Selection." *Journal of Criminal Justice*, 24(1):71–88.

Funk and Wagnall's New International Dictionary. 1995. Chicago, IL: J. G. Ferguson Publishing Company.

Grau, J. J. 1996. "Technology and Criminal Justice." In *Visions for Change: Crime and Justice in the Twenty-first Century*, R. Muraskin and A. R. Roberts, eds. Upper Saddle River, NJ: Prentice Hall. 255–271.

Harer, M. D., and D. J. Steffensmeier. 1996. "Race and Prison Violence." *Criminology*, 34(3):323–355.

Holten, N. G., and L. L. Lamar. 1991. *The Criminal Courts: Structures, Personnel, and Processes*. New York: McGraw-Hill.

Jackson, J. E., and S. Ammen. 1996. "Race and Correctional Officers' Punitive Attitudes toward Treatment Programs for Inmates." *Journal of Criminal Justice*, 24(2):153–166.

Jeffery, C. R. 1956. "The Structure of American Criminological Thinking." *Journal of Criminal Law, Criminology, and Police Science, 49*:533–552.

Johnson, Herbert A., and Nancy Travis Wolfe. 1996. *History of Criminal Justice*, 2d ed. Cincinnati, OH: Anderson Publishing.

Johnson, I., and R. T. Sigler. 1996. "Public Perceptions of Interpersonal Violence." *Journal of Criminal Justice, 24*(5):419–430.

Joo, H.-J., S. Ekland-Olson, and W. R. Kelly. 1995. "Recidivism among Paroled Property Offenders Released during a Period of Prison Reform." *Criminology, 33*(3):389–410.

Kerstetter, W. A., K. A. Rasinski, and C. L. Heiert. 1996. "The Impact of Race on the Investigation of Excessive Force Allegations against Police." *Journal of Criminal Justice, 24*(1):1–16.

Kolstad, A. 1996. "Imprisonment as Rehabilitation: Offenders' Assessment of Why It Does Not Work." *Journal of Criminal Justice, 24*(4):323–337.

Lanier, M. M., and S. Gates. 1996. "An Empirical Assessment of the AIDS Risk Reduction Model (ARRM) Employing Ordered Probit Analyses." *Journal of Criminal Justice, 24*(6):537–548.

Lee, R. D., Jr. 1996. "Prisoners' Rights to Recreation: Quantity, Quality, and Other Aspects." *Journal of Criminal Justice, 24*(2):167–178.

Levine, J. P. 1996. "The Case Study as a Jury Research Methodology." *Journal of Criminal Justice, 24*(4):351–360.

Levine, J. P., M. C. Musheno, and D. J. Palumbo. 1986. *Criminal Justice in America: Law in Action*. New York: John Wiley.

MacKenzie, D. L., R. Brame, D. McDowall, and C. Souryal. 1995. "Boot Camp Prisons and Recidivism in Eight States." *Criminology, 33*(3):327–358.

Maher, L., and K. Daly. 1996. "Women in the Street-Level Drug Economy: Continuity or Change?" *Criminology, 34*(4):465–491.

Madriz, E. 1996. "A Perception of Risk in the Workplace: A Test of Routine Activity Theory." *Journal of Criminal Justice, 24*(5):407–418.

Marvel, T. B., and C. E. Moody. 1995. "The Impact of Enhanced Prison Terms for Felonies Committed with Guns." *Criminology, 33*(2):247–282.

McCoy, H. V., J. D. Wooldredge, F. T. Cullen, P. J. Dubeck, and S. L. Browning. 1996. "Lifestyles of the Old and Not So Fearful: Life Situation and Older Persons' Fear of Crime." *Journal of Criminal Justice,* 24(3):191–206.

McNeece, C. A. 1994. "National Trends in Offense and Case Dispositions." In *Critical Issues in Crime and Justice,* A. R. Roberts, ed. Thousand Oaks, CA: Sage Publications, 157–170.

Meeth, L. R. 1978. "Interdisciplinary Studies." *Change, 10*(7):10.

Muraskin, R., and A. R. Roberts, eds. 1996. *Visions for Change: Crime and Justice in the Twenty-first Century.* Upper Saddle River, NJ: Prentice Hall.

Mutchnick, R. J. 1989. "Criminal Justice Education: Miles to Go before We Sleep." *Quarterly Journal of Ideology, 3*(2):23–34.

Myren, Richard A. 1979. "Criminology and Criminal Justice: Definitions, Trends, and the Future—The Second View." *Two Views of Criminology and Criminal Justice: Definitions, Trends, and the Future.* Joint Commission on Criminology and Criminal Justice Education and Standards, 23–38.

Newman, D. J., and P. R. Anderson. 1989. *Introduction to Criminal Justice,* 4th ed. New York: Random House.

Ogle, R. S., D. Maier-Katkin, and T. J. Bernard. 1995. "A Theory of Homicidal Behavior among Women." *Criminology, 23*(2):173–194.

Pelfrey, W. V. 1980. *The Evolution of Criminology.* Cincinnati, OH: Anderson Publishing Co.

Purpura, P. P. 1997. *Criminal Justice: An Introduction.* Boston: Butterworth-Heinemann.

Quinn, J. F., J. E. Holman, and P. M. Tobolowsky. 1992. "A Case Study Method for Teaching Theoretical Criminology." *Journal of Criminal Justice Education*, 3(1):53–69.

Reasons, C. E., ed. 1974. *The Criminologist: Crime and the Criminal.* Pacific Palisades: Goodyear.

Reed, G. E., and P. C. Yeager. 1996. "Organizational Offending and Neoclassical Criminology: Challenging the Reach of a General Theory of Crime." *Criminology, 34*(3):357–382.

Reichel, P. L. 1982. "A Criminal Activities Checklist." *Teaching Sociology*, 10(1):94–97.

Roberts, A. R. 1994. "Crime in America: Trends, Costs, and Remedies." In *Critical Issues in Crime and Justice*, A. R. Roberts, ed. Thousand Oaks, CA: Sage Publications, 4–18.

Rogers, J. W. 1986. "Teaching Criminology." *Teaching Sociology*, 14(4):257–262.

Schmalleger, F. 1996. *Criminology Today*. Englewood Cliffs, NJ: Prentice Hall.

Schmalleger, F. 1997. *Criminal Justice Today: An Introductory Text for the 21st Century*, 4th ed. Englewood Cliffs, NJ: Prentice Hall.

Schneider, A. L., L. Ervin, and Z. Synder-Joy. 1996. "Further Exploration of the Flight from Discretion: The Role of Risk/Need Instruments in Probation Supervision Decisions." *Journal of Criminal Justice*, 24(2):109–121.

Senna, J. J., and L. J. Seigel. 1996. *Introduction to Criminal Justice*, 6th ed. St. Paul, MN: West Publishing Co.

Simpson, S. S., and L. Elis. 1995. "Doing Gender: Sorting Out the Caste and Crime Conundrum." *Criminology*, 33(1):47–82.

Smith, C., and T. P. Thornberry. 1995. "The Relationship between Childhood Maltreatment and Adolescent Involvement in Delinquency." *Criminology*, 33(4):451–482.

Sourcebook of Criminal Justice Statistics 1995. Washington, D.C.: United States Government Printing Office.

Stohr, M. K., N. P. Lovrich, and M. J. Wood. 1996. "Service Versus Security Concerns in Contemporary Jails: Testing General Difference in Training Topic Assessments." *Journal of Criminal Justice*, 24(5):437–448.

Stokes, L. D., and J. F. Scott. 1996. "Affirmative Action and Selected Minority Groups in Law Enforcement." *Journal of Criminal Justice*, 24(1):29–38.

Storch, J. E., and R. Panzarella. 1996. "Police Stress: State-Trait Anxiety in Relation to Occupational and Personal Stressors." *Journal of Criminal Justice*, 24(2):99–108.

Sutherland, E., and D. Cressey. 1960. *Principles of Criminology*, 7th ed. Philadelphia: J. B. Lippincott Company.

Triplett, R., J. L. Mullings, and K. E. Scarborough. 1996. "Work-Related Stress and Coping among Correctional Officers: Implications from Organizational Literature." *Journal of Criminal Justice*, 24(4):291–308.

Ulmer, J. T., and J. H. Kramer. 1996. "Court Communities under Sentencing Guidelines: Dilemmas of Formal Rationality and Sentencing Disparity." *Criminology*, 34(3):383–408.

Vaughn, M. S. 1996. "Prison Civil Liability for Inmate-against-Inmate Assault and Breakdown/Disorganization Theory. *Journal of Criminal Justice*, 24(2):139–152.

Waldron, R. J. 1989. *The Criminal Justice System: An Introduction*, 4th ed. Philadelphia: Harper and Row.

Warr, M. 1996. "Organization and Instigation in Delinquent Groups." *Criminology*, 34(1):11–38.

Weitzer, R. 1996. "Racial Discrimination in the Criminal Justice System: Findings and Problems in the Literature." *Journal of Criminal Justice*, 24(4):309–322.

Wellford, C. F,. and B. L. Ingraham. 1994. "White Collar Crime: Prevalence, Trends, and Costs." In *Critical Issues in Crime and Justice*, A. R. Roberts, ed. Thousand Oaks, CA: Sage Publications, 77–90.

Bibliography

Adler, Freda, Gerhard O. W. Mueller, and William S. Laufer. *Criminology.* New York: McGraw-Hill, 1991.

Adler, Freda, Gerhard O. W. Mueller, and William S. Laufer. *Criminal Justice: The Core.* New York: McGraw-Hill, 1996.

Adler, Patricia A., and Peter Adler. *Constructions of Deviance: Social Power, Context, and Interaction.* Belmont, CA: Wadsworth, 1994.

Albanese, Jay S., and Robert D. Pursley. *Crime in America: Some Existing and Emerging Issues.* Englewood Cliffs, NJ: Prentice Hall, 1993.

Barak, Gregg, ed. *Varieties of Criminology: Readings from a Dynamic Discipline.* Westport, CT: Praeger, 1994.

Barak-Glantz, Israel L., and Elmer H. Johnson, eds. *Comparative Criminology.* Vol. 31, Sage Research Series in Criminology, Michael R. Gottfredson, ser. ed. Beverly Hills, CA: Sage Publications, 1983.

Bartol, Curt R. *Criminal Behavior: A Psychosocial Approach,* 3rd ed. Englewood Cliffs, NJ: Prentice Hall, 1991.

Bartollas, Clemens, and Loras Jeager. *American Criminal Justice.* New York: Macmillan Publishing, 1988.

Bartollas, Clemens, and Simon Dinitz. *Introduction to Criminology: Order and Disorder.* New York: Harper & Row, 1989.

Best, Joel, and David F. Luckenbill. *Organizing Deviance.* Englewood Cliffs, NJ: Prentice Hall, 1982.

Bohm, Robert M., and Keith N. Haley. *Introduction to Criminal Justice.* New York: McGraw-Hill, 1997.

Brantingham, Paul J., and Patricia L. Brantingham, eds. *Environmental Criminology.* Beverly Hills, CA: Sage Publications, 1981.

Cohen, Bruce J., ed. *Crime In America,* 2d ed. Itasca, IL: F. E. Peacock Publishers, 1977.

Cole, George F. *Criminal Justice: Laws and Politics,* 4th ed. Monterey, CA: Brooks/Cole Publishing, 1994.

Cole, George F. *The American System of Criminal Justice,* 7th ed. New York: Wadsworth Publishing, 1995.

Conrad, John P., and Richard A. Myren. *Two Views of Criminology and Criminal Justice: Definitions, Trends, and the Future.* Prepared for the Joint Commission on Criminology and Criminal Justice Education and Standards, 1979.

Currie, Elliott. *Confronting Crime: An American Challenge.* New York: Pantheon Books, 1985.

Davis, Nanette J., and Clarice Stasz. *Social Control of Deviance: A Critical Perspective.* New York: McGraw-Hill, 1990.

Downes, David, and Paul Rock. *Understanding Deviance: A Guide to the Sociology of Crime and Rule Breaking,* 2d ed. Oxford: Clarendon Press, 1988.

Dudley, William, ed. *Crime and Criminals.* Opposing Viewpoints Series, David L. Bender and Bruno Leone, ser. eds. San Diego: Greenhaven Press, 1989.

Eskridge, Chris W. *Criminal Justice: Concepts and Issues.* Los Angeles: Roxbury Publishing, 1993.

Eysenck, Hans J., and Gisli H. Gudjonsonn. *The Causes and Cures of Criminality.* New York: Plenum Press, 1989.

Farrington, David P., and Roger Tarling, eds. *Prediction in Criminology.* Albany, NY: State University Press, 1985.

Fraenkel, Jack R. *Inquiry into Crucial American Problems.* Crime and Criminals Series, Jack R. Fraenkel, ser. ed. Englewood Cliffs, NJ: Prentice Hall, 1970.

Galliher, John F. *Deviant Behavior and Human Rights.* Englewood Cliffs, NJ: Prentice Hall, 1991.

Gibbons, Don C. *The Criminological Enterprise: Theories and Perspectives.* Englewood Cliffs, NJ: Prentice Hall, 1979.

Gibbons, Don C. *Society, Crime, and Criminal Behavior,* 5th ed. Englewood Cliffs, NJ: Prentice Hall, 1987.

Hancock, Barry W., and Paul M. Sharp. *Criminal Justice in America: Theory, Practice, and Policy.* Upper Saddle River, NJ: Prentice Hall, 1996.

Haskell, Martin R., and Lewis Yablonsky. *Criminology: Crime and Criminality.* Chicago: Rand McNally, 1974.

Hirschi, Travis, and Michael Gottfredson, eds. *Understanding Crime: Current Theory and Research.* Vol. 18, Sage Research Progress Series in Criminology, Michael Gottfredson, ser. ed. Beverly Hills, CA: Sage Publications, 1980.

Holman, John E., and John F. Quinn. *Criminal Justice: Principles and Perspectives.* New York: West Publishing, 1995.

Inciardi, James A., ed. *Radical Criminology: The Coming Crises.* Beverly Hills, CA: Sage Publications, 1980.

Inciardi, James A. *Criminal Justice,* 5th ed. Fort Worth, TX: Harcourt Brace College Publishers, 1996.

Inciardi, James A. *Examining the Justice Process.* New York: Harcourt Brace College Publishers, 1996.

Jackson, Nicky Ali. *Shaping Tomorrow's System.* Contemporary Issues in Criminal Justice Series. New York: McGraw-Hill, 1995.

Jacob, Herbert. *Crime and Justice in Urban America.* Englewood Cliffs, NJ: Prentice Hall, 1980.

Jacoby, Joseph E., ed. *Classics of Criminology.* Oak Park, IL: Moore Publishing Compnay, 1979.

Kaplan, John, and Jerome H. Skolnick. *Criminal Justice: Introductory Cases and Materials,* 4th ed. Mineola, NY: The Foundation Press, 1987.

Kappler, Victor E., Mark Blumberg, and Gary W. Potter. *The Mythology of Crime and Criminal Justice*, 2d ed. Prospect Heights, IL: Waveland Press, 1996.

Klofas, John, and Stan Stojkovic. *Crime and Justice in the Year 2010*. The Wadsworth Contemporary Issues in Crime and Justice Series, Roy Roberg, ser. ed. New York: Wadsworth Publishing, 1995.

Leon, Gloria Rakita. *Case Histories of Deviant Behavior: A Social Learning Analysis*. Boston: Holbrook Press, 1974.

Levine, James P., Michael C. Musheno, and Dennis J. Palumbo. *Criminal Justice in America: Law in Action*. New York: John Wiley and Sons, 1986.

Lilly, J. Robert, Francis T. Cullen, and Richard A. Ball. *Criminological Theory: Context and Consequences*, 2d ed. Thousand Oaks, CA: Sage Publications, 1995.

Lillyquist, Michael J. *Understanding and Changing Criminal Behavior*. Englewood Cliffs, NJ: Prentice Hall, 1980.

Liska, Allen E. *Perspectives on Deviance*, 2d ed. Englewood Cliffs, NJ: Prentice Hall, 1987.

Lurigio, Arthur J., Wesley G. Skogan, and Robert C. Davis, eds. *Victims of Crime: Problems, Policies, and Programs*. Vol. 25, Sage Criminal Justice System Annuals. London: Sage Publications, 1990.

Martin, Randy, Robert J. Mutchnick, and W. Timothy Austin. *Criminological Thought: Pioneers Past and Present*. New York: Macmillan Publishing, 1990.

Masters, Ruth, and Cliff Roberson. *Inside Criminology*. Englewood Cliffs, NJ: Prentice Hall, 1990.

Matthews, Roger, and Jock Young, eds. *Issues in Realist Criminology*. London: Sage Publications, 1992.

McDowell, Charles P. *Criminal Justice: A Community Relations Approach*. Cincinnati, OH: Anderson Publishing, 1984.

McGuigan, Patrick B., and Jon S. Pascale, eds. *Crime and Punishment in Modern America*. Lanham, MD: University Press of America, 1986.

Meier, Robert F., ed. *Theory In Criminology: Contemporary Views*. Vol. 1, Sage Research Progress Series in Criminology, James Inciardi, ser. ed. Beverly Hills, CA: Sage Publications, 1977.

Meier, Robert F. *Crime and Society.* Boston: Allyn and Bacon, 1977.

Michalowski, Raymond J. *Order, Law, and Crime: An Introduction to Criminology.* New York: Random House, 1985.

Nelken, David, ed. *The Futures of Criminology.* London: Sage Publications, 1994.

Nettler, Gwynne. *Explaining Crime.* New York: McGraw-Hill, 1974.

Nettler, Gwynne. *Criminology Lessons: Arguments about Crime, Punishment and the Interpretation of Conduct with Advice for Individuals and Prescriptions for Public Policy.* Cincinnati, OH: Anderson Publishing Company, 1989.

Newman, Donald J., and Patrick R. Anderson. *Introduction to Criminal Justice*, 4th ed. New York: West Publishing, 1989.

Palmer, Stuart, and John A. Humphrey. *Deviant Behavior: Patterns, Sources, and Control.* New York: Plenum Press, 1990.

Pelfrey, William V. *The Evolution of Criminology.* Cincinnati, OH: Anderson Publishing, 1980.

Pepinsky, Harold E. *Rethinking Criminology.* Vol. 27, Sage Research Progress Series in Criminology, Michael R. Gottfredson, ser. ed. Beverly Hills, CA: Sage Publications, 1982.

Regoli, Robert M., and John D. Hewitt. *Criminal Justice.* Englewood Cliffs, NJ: Prentice Hall, 1996.

Sagarin, Edward, ed. *Criminology: New Concerns, Essays in Honor of Hans W. Mattick.* Beverly Hills, CA: Sage Publications, 1979.

Sagarin, Edward, ed. *Taboos in Criminology.* Vol. 15, Sage Research Progress Series in Criminology, James A. Inciardi, ser. ed. Beverly Hills, CA: Sage Publications, 1980.

Samaha, Joel. *Criminal Justice*, 4th ed. New York: West Publishing. 1997.

Schmalleger, Frank. *Criminal Justice Today*, 4th ed. Upper Saddle River, NJ: Prentice Hall, 1997.

Senna, Joseph, and Larry Seigel. *Introduction to Criminal Justice*, 7th ed. New York: West Publishing, 1996.

Sheley, Joseph F. *America's "Crime Problem": An Introduction to Criminology.* Belmont, CA: Wadsworth Publishing, 1985.

Sheley, Joseph F. *Exploring Crime: Readings in Criminology and Criminal Justice.* Belmont, CA: Wadsworth Publishing, 1987.

Sheley, Joseph F. *Criminology.* Belmont, CA: Wadsworth Publishing, 1991.

Seigel, Larry J., ed. *American Justice: Research of the National Institute of Justice.* New York: West Publishing, 1980.

Siegel, Larry J. *Criminology,* 2d ed. St. Paul, MN: West Publishing, 1986.

Sullivan, John J., and Joseph L. Victor, eds. *Criminal Justice.* Annual Editions. Guilford, CT: Dushkin Publishing, 1992.

Sullivan, John J., and Joseph L. Victor, eds. *Criminal Justice.* Annual Editions. Guilford, CT: Dushkin Publishing, 1993.

Sullivan, John J., and Joseph L. Victor, eds. *Criminal Justice.* Annual Editions. Guilford, CT: Dushkin Publishing, 1994.

Sullivan, John J., and Joseph L. Victor, eds. *Criminal Justice.* Annual Editions. Guilford, CT: Dushkin Publishing, 1995.

Szumski, Bonnie, ed. *Criminal Justice.* Opposing Viewpoints Series, David L. Bender and Bruno Leone, ser. eds. San Diego: Greenhaven Press, 1987.

Territo, Leonard, James B. Halsted, and Max Bromley. *Crime and Justice in America*, 4th ed. New York: West Publishing, 1992.

Timmer, Doug A., and Stanley D. Eitzen. *Crime in the Streets and Crime in the Suites: Perspectives on Crime and Criminal Justice.* Boston: Allyn and Bacon, 1989.

Toch, Hans, ed. *Psychology of Crime and Criminal Justice.* New York: Holt, Rinehart, and Winston, 1979.

Vito, Gennaro F., and Ronald M. Holmes. *Criminology: Theory, Research, and Policy.* Belmont, CA: Wadsworth Publishing, 1994.

Voigt, Lydia, William E. Thornton Jr., Leo Barrile, and Jerrol M. Seaman. *Criminology and Justice.* New York: McGraw-Hill, 1994.

Vold, George B., and Thomas J. Bernard. *Theoretical Criminology,* 3rd ed. New York: Oxford University Press, 1986.

Walker, Samuel. *Sense and Nonsense about Crime: A Policy Guide,* 3rd ed. Pacific Grove, CA: Brooks/Cole Publishing Company, 1989.

Weston, Paul B., and Kenneth M. Wells. *The Administration of Justice,* 5th ed. Englewood Cliffs, NJ: Prentice Hall, 1987.

Williams, Frank P. III, and Marilyn D. McShane. *Criminological Theory: Selected Classic Readings.* Cincinnati, OH: Anderson Publishing Co, 1993.

Williams, Frank P. III, and Marilyn D. McShane. *Criminological Theory,* 2nd ed. Englewood Cliffs, NJ: Prentice Hall, 1994.

Wilson, James Q. *Thinking About Crime.* New York: Random House, 1975.

Wilson, James Q., and Richard J. Herrnstein. *Crime and Human Nature.* New York: Simon and Schuster, 1985.

Wilson, James Q., and Joan Petersilia, eds. *Crime.* San Francisco: ICS Press, 1995.

Winfree, L. Thomas, Jr., and Howard Abadinsky. *Understanding Crime: Theory and Practice.* Chicago: Nelson-Hall, 1996.

Yablonsky, Lewis. *Criminology: Crime and Criminality,* 4th ed. New York: Harper and Row, 1990.

Index

Other Criminal Justice Books from Butterworth-Heinemann

Contemporary Criminal Law
David T. Skelton
1997   400pp   pb   0-7506-9811-X

Criminal Investigation: Law and Practice
Michael F. Brown
1997   368pp   pb   0-7506-9665-6

Criminal Justice: An Introduction
Philip P. Purpura
1996   400pp   pb   0-7506-9630-3

Criminal Justice Statistics: A Practical Approach
Arthur J. Lurigio, M.L. Dantzker, Magnus J. Seng, and James M. Sinacore
1996   296pp   hc   0-7506-9672-9

Juvenile Justice System, The: Law and Process
Mary Clement
1996   345pp   hc   0-7506-9810-1

Detailed information on these and all other BH-Criminal Justice titles may be found in the our catalog(Item #800). To request a copy, call 1-800-366-2665. You can also visit our web site at: http://www.bh.com

These books are available from all good bookstores or in case of difficulty call:
1-800-366-2665 in the U.S. or +44-1865-310366 in Europe.

E-Mail Mailing List
An e-mail mailing list giving information on latest releases, special promotions/ offers and other news relating to Butterworth-Heinemann Criminal Justice titles is available. To subscribe, send an e-mail message to majordomo@world.std.com. Include in message body (not in subject line) subscribe bh-criminal-justice